Windows to the Past

Windows to the Past

ROBERT DEUTSCH MICHAEL HELTZER

ARCHAEOLOGICAL CENTER PUBLICATION
TEL AVIV-JAFFA ISRAEL
1997

ARCHAEOLOGICAL CENTER PUBLICATION
7 Mazal Dagim street
Old City of Jaffa 68036 Israel
Phone: (972) 3 682-6243 Fax: (972) 3 681-6837

ISBN 965–222–839–7

Printed in Israel
at "Graphit" Ltd., Jerusalem

CONTENTS

ACKNOWLEDGEMENTS

This is our third book[1] motivated by the desire to enrich our historic and linguistic knowledge of the most exciting period in the Jewish history, the Old Testament period.

Silent epigraphic evidence kept in private collections are presented here and brought up to common knowledge.

The present publication is another rescue-work, saving historical information about Israel and the Middle East from being lost.

The material published in this study, comes from six private collectors and two licensed antiquity dealers. We would like to express our gratitude for allowing us to publish the material.

Drawings by Rodica Pinchas and Robert Deutsch, photos by Zeev Radovan and Pavel Shrago.

Robert Deutsch Michael Heltzer

COLLECTIONS

Collection no.1 — (Mr. Sh. Moussaieff, London) Arrowheads: 81, 82, 83, 84; Bullae: 92, 93a,b, 94a,b,c; Seals: 97, 98, 99, 100, 101, 103, 104, 106, 107, 108, 109, 110, 111: Handles: 114, 115; Weight: 120

Collection no. 2 — (Mr. L. Wolfe, Jerusalem) Bullae: 85, 86, 87, 88, 89, 90, 95

Collection no.3 — (Mr. Ch. Kaufman, Antwerpen) Arrowhead: 80; Bullae: 91, 96; Measurement Juglet: 113

Collection no.6 — (Mr. Oded Golan, Tel Aviv) Storage jar: 112.

Collection no.7 — (Ex. Mr. A. Saeedi, London) Seal: 102

Collection no.11 — (Mr. Gil Chaya, Geneva) Seal: 105, Weights: 117, 118

Collection no.12 — (Mr. N. Meron, Jerusalem) Seal impression: 116

Collection no. 13 — (Mr. Sh. Qedar, Jerusalem) Weight: 119

---

1 The previous two books are: *Forty New Ancient West Semitic Inscriptions*. 1994, Tel Aviv-Jaffa and *New Epigraphic Evidence from the Biblical Period*. 1995, Tel Aviv-Jaffa.

FIVE INSCRIBED ARROWHEADS

In our previous two published books (Deutsch and Heltzer, 1994:11–21; 1995:11–38) we dealt with 14 Canaanite-Phoenician inscribed arrowheads, bringing the total number of inscribed arrowheads recorded to date to 43. Meanwhile the inscribed arrowhead: *ḥṣ swr // ʾš ʿbdy* "Arrow of Suwar, man (retainer) of ʿAbday", has been published (Cross, 1996), mentioned in our previous book (Deutsch and Heltzer, 1995:27, No.XXXIV).

Five additional inscribed arrowheads of unknown provenance which are kept in private collections are presented here rising the number of such inscribed arrowheads to 48.[1]

We continue the numbering from where we left off in our last book:

80.(15). **Bronze arrowhead blade** (Fig.80), of elliptic shape (Cross and Milik, 1956:17, type XII). The tang is missing. Its length is 5.9 cm., and its blade width is 1.4 cm., inscribed on both sides. The letters consist of short lines struck by a chisel. The inscription is damaged in some areas by corrosion, but the reading is certain.

The inscription reads:

> **חץ אלמלך // רב מכרם**
> *ḥṣ ʾlmlk // rb mkrm*
> "Arrow of ʾElimelek, chief of *mkrm* (merchants, traders)"

The letter *ṣ* (*ṣade*) has an archaic form and the letter ʾ (*alef*) has a mirror shape. Moreover, the two letters *l* (lamed) are written upside down. These unestablished features of the letters point toward an early date, i.e. the middle of the eleventh century B.C.E.

The name *ʾElimelek* appears in the book of Ruth in the OT (1:2,3; 2:1,3; 4:3,9). In Phoenician it had possibly the vocalization **Ilumilku* or

---

1 The source of all five arrowheads is Lebanon and they were acquired on the antiquities markets in Europe. They are presently kept in two private collection: Mr. Ch. Kaufman of Antwerpen (No.80) and Mr. S. Moussaieff of London (Nos. 81–84) who kindly gave us the permission to publish them.

**Ilumilki*, lit. "God ʾEl (ʾIl) is my (the) King, or My God is Milk(u)". The name is known from Ugaritic texts (Del Olmo Lete and Sanmartin, 1996:28), from the El-Amarna letters and Alalakh texts (Hess, 1993:86–88), as also in the West-Semitic texts of the first millennium B.C. (Fales, 1986, No.23; Maraqten, 1988:69).

rb — "chief", "commander", "supervisor". In this meaning the term *rb* appears in the OT, in Phoenician and Punic, Ugaritic and also on another arrowhead: *ḥṣ bnyʾ* // *rb ʾlf* "Arrow of Banayaʾ, chief of thousand" (Cross, 1992, No.2, 1993, No.7, 1996, No.22; Deutsch and

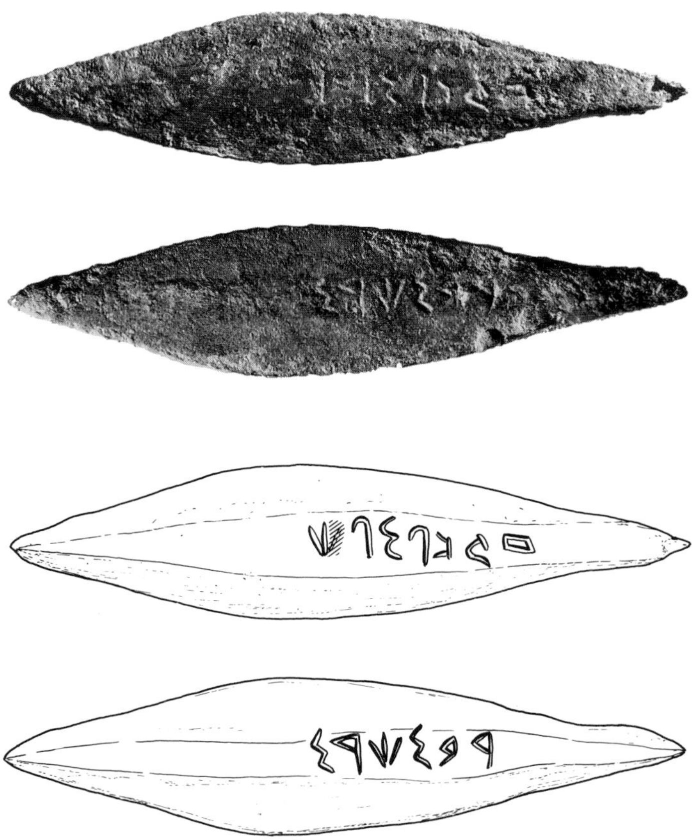

Ch. Kaufman collection

Fig. 80. Arrowhead belonging to "ʾElimelek, chief of merchants (traders)"

Heltzer 1995:26, XXIV). In the administrative text of Ugarit the term *rb* appears as the title of an official supervisor, a person in charge over a professional group of *bnš mlk* "royal men", i.e. dependent royal servicemen (Heltzer, 1982:211).

mkrm — (pl. masc.) This word in the meaning "merchant", "trader" is attested in Punic (CIS I 407, 334, 3885, 4874 etc) and in Ugaritic, where the *mkrm* were royal merchants organized also in a professional group (Heltzer, 1978:121–147). There are also the Old Babylonian, Old Assyrian and Alalakh texts of the first half of the second millennium B.C.E. where we find the *UGULA / wakil tamkārum*, (AHW 1456b, 6e). We have here a fully new feature in the Southern Levant at the middle of the XI century B.C.E. were the *mkrm*, an independent group, who probably united their individual efforts for common trade-expeditions and took care for their security at their routes, or it was an organization, submitted to some kind of authority and the *rb* was the imposed "chief"?. The historical value of this inscription is certain.

81.(16). **Bronze arrowhead** (Fig.81), of spatulate shape (Cross and Milik, 1956:17, type XI). Its length is 9.4 cm., and its blade width is 1.9 cm. The tang is slightly bent. Inscribed on both sides. The letters inscribed on the side bearing the owners name, consist of short lines struck deep by a chisel, while the inscription on the side bearing the patronymic consists of lines struck weakly and carelessly also by a chisel, as if two scribes were involved in the writing. The arrowhead is in good state of preservation except some area damaged by corrosion, yet, the reading is certain. All the letters are written in the correct direction. This points toward a date in the first half of the 10th century B.C.E.

The inscription reads:

חץ עבדי // בׄן מלכרם
ḥṣ ʿbdy // b̊n mlkrm
"Arrow of ʿAbday, son of Malkiram"

ʿbdy — Cf. next arrowhead below.

mlkrm — "My King (epitheton of God) is high, exalted". The name *Mlkrm* is known in Phoenician and Punic inscriptions (Benz, 1972:140). There is an important inscribed fragment of a Phoenician bronze bowl of the VIII cent. B.C.E. with the inscription *lḥlṣ ʿbd mlkrm* "Belonging to Ḥeleṣ, servant of Malkiram" (Loewenstamm, 1958:159–160). Cf. also *Mlkyrm*, the son of Yekonyā, the king of Judah (I Chr. 3:18). The name appears in its full spelling on another arrowhead *ḥṣ mlkyrm* / / *bn ʿbdy* "Arrow of Malkiram, son of ʿAbday" (Deutsch and Heltzer, 1995:17, No.44). Therefore, it is possible that we have here two arrowheads with the names of three generations *mlkyrm* — *ʿbdy* — *mlkrm*.

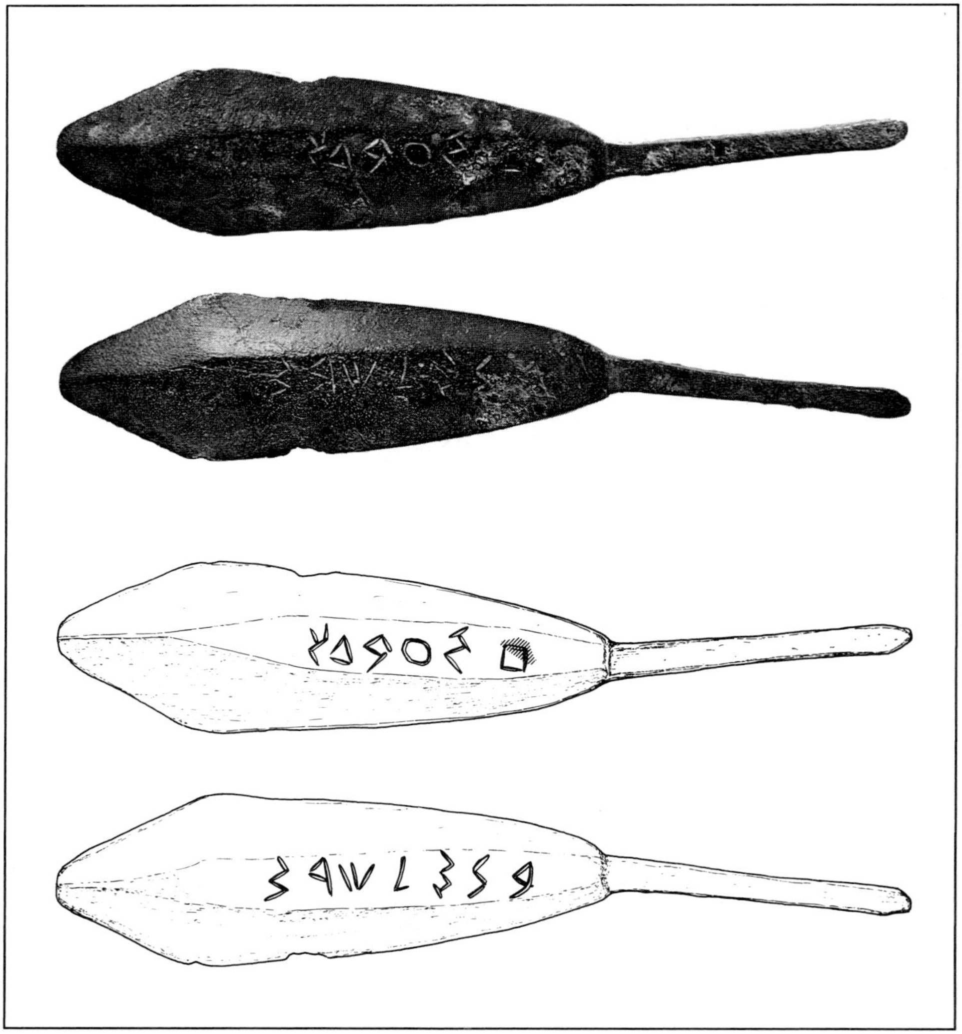

Fig. 81. Arrowhead belonging to "ʿAbday, son of Malkiram"

82.(17).　　**Bronze arrowhead** (Fig.82), of oblong shape (Cross and Milik, 1956:17, type VII). Its length is 8.9 cm., and its blade width is 1.6 cm. The tang is slightly bent. Inscribed on both sides. The letters consist of short lines struck by a chisel. The arrowhead is in good state of preservation except some area damaged by corrosion. All the letters are written in the correct direction. Therefore this arrowhead is to be dated also to the first half of the 10th century B.C.E.

The inscription reads:

חץ אלעם // בן עבדי

ḥṣ ᵓlᶜm // bn ᶜbdy

"Arrow of ᵓElᶜam (or ᵓEliᶜam), son of ᶜAbday"

Sh. Moussaieff collection

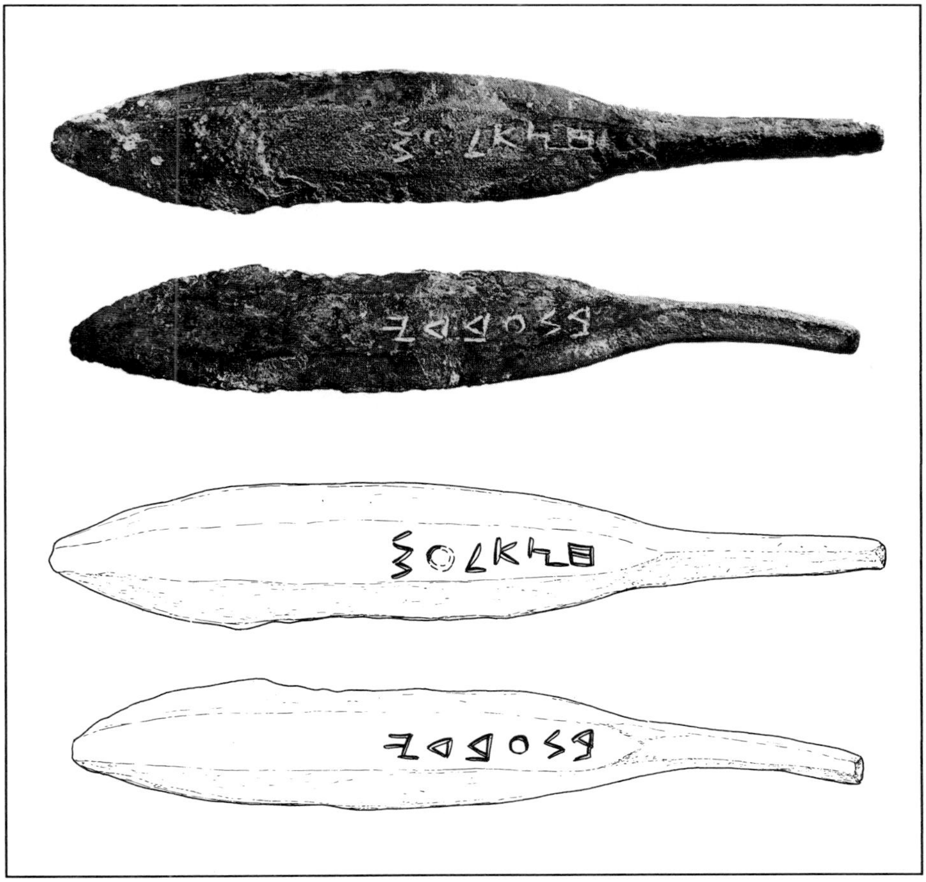

Fig. 82. Arrowhead belonging to "ᵓElᶜam (or ᵓEliᶜam), son of ᶜAbday"

ʾlʿm — the name appears on arrowheads for the first time. ʾEliʿam (ʾlyʿm) is known from the OT (II Sam.11:3; 23:24) as also ʿAmmiʾel (ʿmyʾl) (Num.13:12; Sam.9:4,5; 17:27; Chr.3:5; 26:5). The etymology here is "My God is *ʿm*". The component *ʿAm* appears frequently as the theophoric element in early West Semitic names such as *ʾlhʿm* or *ʿmndb* (Aufrecht, 1989, Nos. 17, 40, 78), *ʾlʿm* (Benz, 1972:61; CIS, I. 147:6). The term ʿm "paternal uncle" appears frequently in almost all semitic languages.

ʿbdy — *ʿAbday*. Hypocoristicon with the element *ʿbd* — servant of (name of deity). *ʿAbday* has emerged as the most frequent name inscribed on Phoenician arrowheads. There are six published arrowheads bearing this name: 1) *ḥṣ kty // mšq ʿbdy*, 2) *ḥṣ ymn // ʾš ʿbdy*, 3) *ḥṣ swr // ʾš ʿbdy*, 4) *ḥṣ mlkyrm // bn ʿbdy*, 5) *ḥṣ mhrn // bn ʿbdy*, 6) *ḥṣ šʾ // bn ʿbdy*. (Deutsch and Heltzer, 1995:26–7, Nos. XXVII, XXXII, XXXIV, XXXIX, XL, XLI; 1997:111; Cross, 1996:9*). To this list we have to add the two arrowheads presented here: 7) *ḥṣ ʿbdy // bn mlkrm* and 8) *ḥṣ ʾlʿm // bn ʿbdy* (Nos. 81 and 82 above).

83.(18). **Bronze arrowhead blade** (Fig.83), length 4.8 cm.; blade width 1.4 cm., of elliptic shape (Cross and Milik, 1956:17, type XII). The arrowhead has been shortened and the tip of the tang is missing. Inscribed on both sides, the letters consist of short lines struck by a chisel. The inscription is damaged in some areas by strokes, but the reading is certain. All the letters are written correctly except for the two letters *n* (*nun*) which are written with a moderate inclination toward right. This points toward a date around 11th century B.C.E.

The inscription reads:

חׄץ עׄזר // בן נׄכר
ḥ̇ṣ ʿ̇zr // bn ṅkr
"Arrow of ʿAzar, son of *Nkr*"

ʿzr — ʿEzer, ʿOzer or ʿAzar: Biblical name (I Chr. 4:4; 7:21; 12:9 etc.), probably a hypocoristicon from the name *ʿazarbaʿal* known from the arrowhead: *ḥṣ ʿzrbʿl // bn ʾdnbʿl* "Arrow of ʿAzarbaʿal, son of ʾAdonibaʿal" (Milik, 1961, No.3). This is the first appearance of the shortened name on arrowheads of the 11th–10th century B.C.E. (Cf. Deutsch and Heltzer, 1994:55–56, No.24 with the discussion).

bn nkr — "Son of *Nkr*": The name is unknown from the OT. (Cf. Phoen. Ugar. Aram. S. Ar. Ammon.). The root *nkr* means in Hebrew "to be alien", "to be unrecognized", as also *nokrī* means "a foreigner", "belonging to another society". Therefore it is possible to treat this name as a nickname "the son of the foreigner, stranger". We have seen, that among the owners of arrows where a Kitionian from Cyprus (Deutsch and Heltzer, 1994:16–18), and an Egyptian *Wry* (Deutsch and Heltzer, 1995:13–14), therefore it can be also a *nokrī*"foreigner". Yet, the Aramaic inscription from Sfire in northern Syria from the VIII century B.C.E. (KAI, 222 a:10) mention a god *nkr*. Therefore the *nkr* on our arrowhead can be also a hypocoristic theophoric name but such proposal is unlikely.

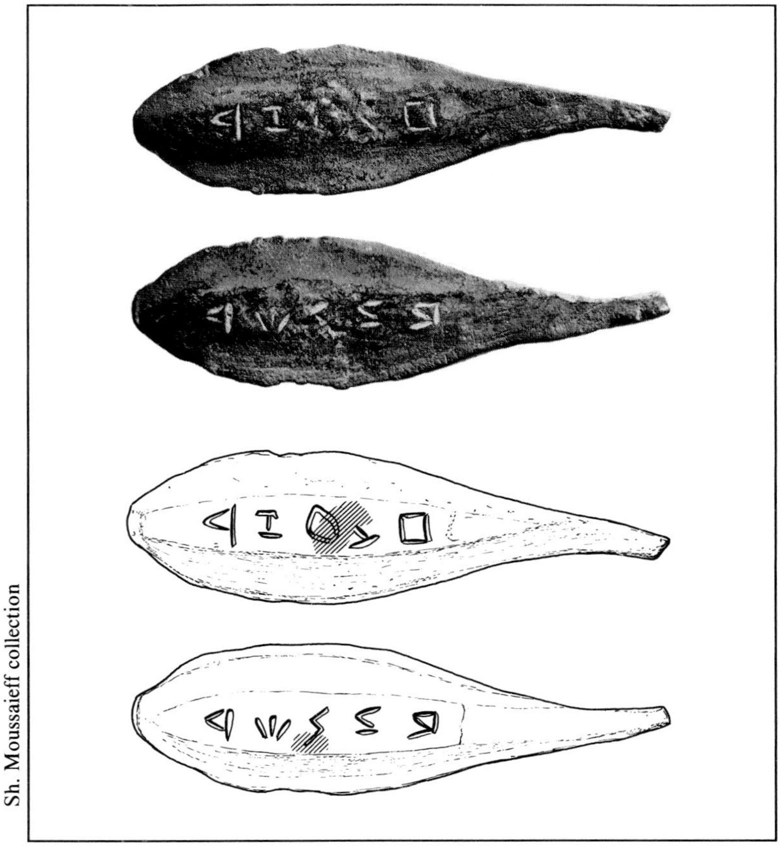

Fig. 83. Arrowhead belonging to "ʿAzar, son of *Nkr*"

84.(19). **Bronze arrowhead** (Fig.84), of spatulate shape (Cross and Milik, 1956:17, type XI). Its length is 7.2 cm., and its blade width is 1.4 cm. Inscribed on both sides, the letters consist of short lines struck by a chisel. The inscription is damaged in some areas by corrosion and only the name of the owner is certain. This arrowhead is dated according to the shape of the letters to the first half of the 10th century B.C.E.

The inscription reads:

חץ זכר׳ // בן׳..ש..
ḥṣ zkṙ // bṅ ..š..
"Arrow of Zakkur, son of ..*š*.."

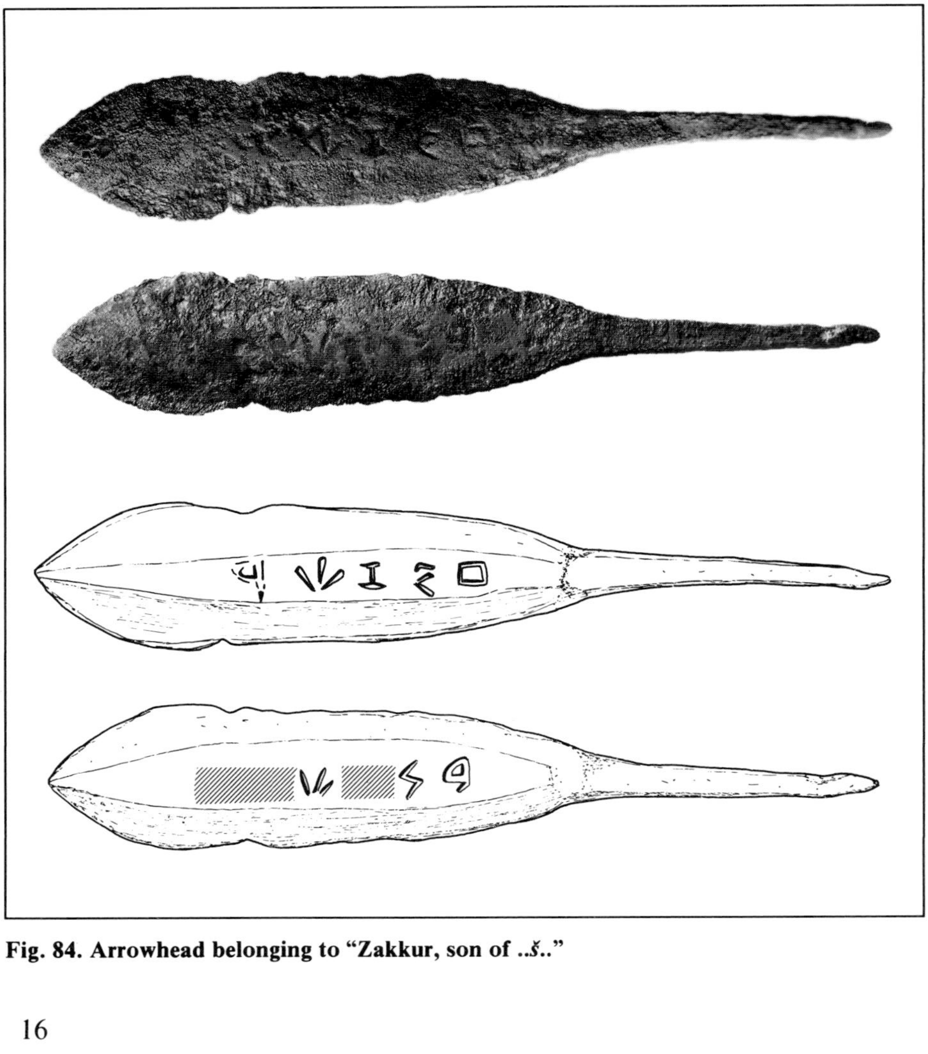

Sh. Moussaieff collection

Fig. 84. Arrowhead belonging to "Zakkur, son of ..*š*.."

Zkr — (*zakir, zakkur* etc.) The root *zkr* is frequent in Hebrew as an element of theophorical name (Num. 13:4, I Chr. 4:26, 8:31; Ezra 8:14; Neh. 3:2 etc.). The name *Zkr* or the root *zkr* is frequent also in Phoenician, Ammonite and Aramaic. It appears on three other arrowheads: *ḥṣ zkrbʿ[l] / / bn bnʿn[t]* "Arrow of Zakarbaʿa[l], son of Ben-ʿAna[t]" (Milik, 1956:3–6) and on two royal arrowheads: *ḥṣ zkrbʿl / / mlk ʾmr* "Arrow of Zakarbaʿal, king of ʾAmurru" (Starcky, 1982:178–186; Deutsch and Heltzer, 1994:12 No.1). The patronym is illegible.

Discussion

The above presented inscribed arrowheads raise the number of such items published up to date to 48. The following, is a list of this apparatus:

I *ḥṣ ʾdʾ (sic. ʾbʾ) / / bn ʿky* "Arrow of ʾIddoʾ, son of ʿAkky"
(Guigues, 1926:325–328; Ronzevalle, 1926:329–358; Mitchell, 1985; Sass, 1988, No.10; Bordreuil, 1992:212, No.I; Cross, 1993:542, No.14, after a reexamination of the arrowhead, reads *ʾbʾ instead of ʾdʾ)*

II *ḥṣ ʿbdlbʾt* "Arrow of ʿAbdlabiʾat"
(Milik-Cross, 1954, No.1; Mitchell, 1985; Sass, 1988, No.2; Bordreuil, 1992:212, No.II; Heltzer, 1992:28, No.IIa; Cross, 1993:542, No.1)

III *ḥṣ ʿbdlbʾt* "Arrow of ʿAbdlabiʾat"
(Milik-Cross, 1954, No.2; Mitchell, 1985; Sass, 1988, No.2; Bordreuil, 1992:212, No.III; Heltzer, 1992:28 No.IIb; Cross, 1993:542, No.2)

IV *ḥṣ ʿbdlbʾt* "Arrow of ʿAbdlabiʾat"
(Milik-Cross, 1954, No.3; Mitchell, 1985; Sass, 1988, No.3; Bordreuil, 1992:212, No.IV; Heltzer, 1992:28 No.IIc)

V *ḥṣ zkrbʿ[l] / / bn bnʿn[t]* "Arrow of Zakarbaʿa[l], son of Ben-ʿAna[t]"
(Milik, 1956:3–6; Mitchell, 1985; Sass, 1988, No.15; Bordreuil, 1992:212, No.V; Heltzer, 1992:29 No.III; Cross, 1993:542, No.15)

VI *ḥṣ grbʿl // ṣdny* "Arrow of Gerbaʿal, the Sidonian"
(Milik, 1961:103–108; Mitchell, 1985, No.7; Sass, 1988, No.7; Bordreuil, 1992:212, No.VI; Heltzer, 1992:29 No.V; Cross, 1993:542, No.10)

VII *ḥṣ ʿzrbʿl // bn ʾdnbʿl* "Arrow of ʿAzarbaʿal, son of ʾAdonibaʿal"
(Milik, 1961, No.3; Mitchell, 1985 No.8; Sass, 1988, No.13; Bordreuil, 1992:212, No.VII; Heltzer, 1992:30 No.VI; Cross, 1993:542, No.18)

VIII *ḥṣ rfʾ // bn yḥš* "Arrow of Rafaʾ, son of Yaḥuš"
(Martin, 1962:175–197; Mitchell, 1985 No.9; Sass, 1988, No.6; Bordreuil, 1992:212, No.VIII; Heltzer, 1992:30 No.VII; Cross, 1993:542, No.9)

IX *ḥṣ ytʾ // bn zmʾ* "Arrow of Yataʾ, son of Zemaʾ"
(SdT, 1980:31; Mitchell, 1985, No.10; Sass, 1988, No.8; Bordreuil, 1992:212, No.IX; Heltzer, 1992:29 No.VIII; Cross, 1993:542, No.6)

X *ḥṣ ʿbdl<b>ʾt* "Arrow of ʿAbdla<bi>at"
(Cross, 1980:4–6; Mitchell, 1985, No.11; Sass, 1988, No.4; Bordreuil, 1992:212, No.X; Heltzer, 1992, No.IId; Cross, 1993:542, No.4)

XI *ʿbdlbʾt // bn ʿnt* "ʿAbdlabiʾat, son of ʿAnat"
(Cross, 1980:6–7; Mitchell, 1985, No.12; Sass, 1988, No.5; Bordreuil, 1992:212, No.XI; Heltzer, 1992, No.IIe; Cross, 1993:542, No.5)

XII *ḥṣ zkrbʿl // mlk ʾmr* "Arrow of Zakarbaʿal, king of ʾAmurru"
(Starcky, 1982:178–186; Mitchell, 1985, No.13; Sass, 1988, No.12; Bordreuil, 1992:213, No.XII; Heltzer, 1992, No.IX; Cross, 1993:542, No.16)

XIII *ḥṣ ʿbdny // ʾš ʿzbʿl* "Arrow of ʿAbdony, man of ʿOzibaʿal"
(Bordreuil, 1982:187–192; 1992:213, No.XIII; Mitchell, 1985, No.14; Sass, 1988, No.9; Heltzer, 1992:31–2 No.X; Cross, 1993:542, No.8)

XIV *ḥṣ ʾdʿ // bn bʿlʾ* "Arrow of ʾAdaʿ, son of Baʿalaʾ"
(Mitchell, 1985, No.15 (20?); Sass, 1988, No. 14; Bordreuil, 1992:213, No.XIV; Heltzer, 1992:32 No.XII; Cross, 1993:542, No.17)

XV *ḥṣ pdy // bn qry* "Arrow of Pady, son of Q[u]/eri"
(Sader, 1990:315–317; Bordreuil, 1992:213, No.XV; Heltzer, 1992:33, No.XIV)

XVI *ḥṣ ywḥnn // ʾš ʿzbʿl* "Arrow of Yawḥanan, man of ʿOzibaʿal"
(Sternberg, 1990:69, No.431, (*ḥṣ .. // ʾš ʿzbʿl*); Cross, 1993:542, No.24)

XVII *ḥṣ ʾdnšʿ // rb* [... "Arrow of ʾAdonišuʿa, commander of [..."
(Tarragon, 1990:245–251; Bordreuil, 1992:213, No.XVI; Cross, 1996, No.18)

XVIII *ḥṣ mhrn // bn yṭl* "Arrow of Maha/iran, son of Yṭl"
(Sternberg and Wolfe, 1989:9, No.1; Lemaire, 1989:53–56; Bordreuil, 1992:213, No.XVII; Heltzer, 1992:33 No.XIII; Cross, 1996, No.15)

XIX *ḥṣ pqḥy // ʾš zrʿy* "Arrow of Paqaḥy, man of Zarʿay"
(Bordreuil, 1992:206 No.XVIII)

XX *ḥṣ šlm bn [..]y* "Arrow of Šallum, son of [..]y"
(Bordreuil, 1992:207 No.XIX; Cross, 1996, No.19)

XXI *ḥṣ bnʾ // ʾš špṭ* "Arrow of Banaʾ, man of Šapaṭ"
(Bordreuil, 1992:207 No.XX; Cross, 1996, No.20)

XXII *ḥṣ ʿzm // bn mlky* "Arrow of ʿAzzam, son of M[a]/ilky"
(Bordreuil, 1992:207 No.XXI; Cross, 1996, No.21)

XXIII *ḥṣ pʾ // b[n ..]* "Arrow of Paʾ, so[n of ..]"
(Bordreuil, 1992:208, No.XXII; Cross, 1996, c* spurious but reads *gʾ* instead of *pʾ*)

XXIV *ḥṣ bnyʾ // rb ʾlf* "Arrow of Banayaʾ, chief of thousand"
(Cross, 1992, No.1; 1996, No.22)

XXV *ḥṣ yšʾ* "Arrow of Yišaʾ"
(Cross, 1992, No.2; 1996, No.23)

XXVI *ḥṣ šmdʿ bn yšbʿ // ʾš šfṭ hṣr* "Arrow of Šemdaʿ, son of Yišbaʿ // man of Šafaṭ the Tyrian"
(Cross, 1992a; 1996, No.24)

XXVII *ḥṣ ymn // ʾš ʿbdy* "Arrow of Yaman, man of ʿAbday"
(Bordreuil, 1982:190; Sass, 1988, No.15; Cross, 1996, a)

XXVIII *ḥṣ šfṭ // bn zmʾ* "Arrow of Šafaṭ, son of Za/emaʾ"
(Cross, 1996, b, spurious)

XXIX *ḥṣ zkrbʿl // mlk ʾmr* "Arrow of Zakarbaʿal, king of ʾAmurru"
(Deutsch and Heltzer, 1994:12 No.1)

XXX *ḥṣ ʾlbʿl // ʾš ydbʿl* "Arrow of Elibaʿal, man of Yadbaʿal"
(Deutsch and Heltzer, 1994:13 No.2)

XXXI *ḥṣ bnʿnt // bn mrṣ* "Arrow of Benʿanat, son of Mereṣ"
(Deutsch and Heltzer, 1994:15 No.3)

XXXII *ḥṣ kty // mšq (sic.) ʿbdy* "Arrow of Kitionian, cupbearer of ʿAbday"
(Deutsch and Heltzer, 1994:16–18, No.4; Cross, 1995; McCarter, 1996; Deutsch and Heltzer, 1997:111–112)

XXXIII *ḥṣ zmʾ // bn ʾlṣʾl* "Arrow of Za/emaʾ, son of ʾEleṣʾel"
(Deutsch and Heltzer, 1994:18, No.5)

XXXIV *ḥṣ swr // ʾš ʿbdy* "Arrow of Suwar, retainer of ʿAbday"
(Cross, 1996)

XXXV *ḥṣ tdbʿl // bn rm* "Arrow of Tadibaʿal, son of Ram"
(Deutsch and Heltzer, 1995:11–12, No.40)

XXXVI *ḥṣ wry*
(Deutsch and Heltzer, 1995:13–14, No.41, no patronym)

XXXVII *ḥṣ šmrm // bn mrdgn* "Arrow of Šemram, son of Mardagan"
(Deutsch and Heltzer, 1995:14–15, No.42)

XXXVIII *ḥṣ ʿbdʾlm // bn ʾky* "Arrow of ʿAbdʾelim, son of ʾAky"
(Deutsch and Heltzer, 1995:16–17, No.43)

XXXIX *ḥṣ mlkyrm // bn ʿbdy* "Arrow of Malkiram (Milkiram), son of ʿAbday"
(Deutsch and Heltzer, 1995:17–18, No.44)

XL *ḥṣ mhrn // bn ʿbdy* "Arrow of Maharan, son of ʿAbday"
(Deutsch and Heltzer, 1995:18–19, No.45)

XLI *ḥṣ šʾ // bn ʿbdy* "Arrow of *Šʾ* son of ʿAbday"
(Deutsch and Heltzer, 1995:20, No.46)

XLII *ḥṣ ʾḥʾ // bn ʾny* "Arrow of ʾAḥaʾ, son of ʾAny"
(Deutsch and Heltzer, 1995:21–22, No.47)

XLIII *ḥṣ ʾḥʾ // bn ʿštrt* "Arrow of ʾAḥaʾ, son of ʿAštart"
(Deutsch and Heltzer, 1995:22–23, No.48)

XLIV *ḥṣ ʾlmlk // rb mkrm* "Arrow of ʾElimelek, chief of merchants"
(cf. No.80 above)

XLV *ḥṣ ʿbdy // bn mlkrm* "Arrow of ʿAbday, son of Malkiram"
(cf. No.81 above)

XLVI *ḥṣ ʾlʿm // bn ʿbdy* "Arrow of ʾEliʿam, son of ʿAbday"
(cf. No.82 above)

XLVII *ḥṣ ʿzr // bn nkr* "Arrow of ʿAzar, son of *Nkr*"
(cf. No.83 above)

XLVIII *ḥṣ zkr // bn ..š..* "Arrow of Zakkur, son of *..š..*"
(cf. No.84 above)

Following our analysis (Deutsch and Heltzer, 1995:28–37), and considering critical remarks expressed by scholars (Cross, 1995:188–189; McCarter, 1996), we reach the following conclusions:

1. The arrows belonged to 47 individuals (Arrowheads XII and XXIX belonged to the king of Amurru).

2. F.M. Cross (1995:188–9) challenged our reading of the arrowhead-inscription *ḥṣ kty // mšl ʿbdy* "Arrow of the Kitian, ruler of ʿbday" (Deutsch and Heltzer, 1994. No.1): Instead of the personal name *ʿbdy* "ʿAbday" Professor Cross argued that the inscription refers to *ʿbdn* "ʿAbdon" which he identified as Khirbet ʿAbdeh, a ruin 5 Km. east of Akhzib in northern Israel, accepted also by A. Lemaire (1995:212) and G. Barkay (personal communication). Cross' main objections to our reading were based on two very different criteria. On one hand, he rejected the idea that an individual named ʿAbday would have a "ruler" attached to him; therefore Cross preferred to understand *ʿbdy* as a place name. On the other, he was misled by the photograph that appears in our original publication. The surface of the arrowhead has been damaged by corrosion and the image was less than one might have desired; therefore he read the final letter of the word in question as *nun* instead of *yod.*

Professor Cross' second objection also cannot be sustained. As a new photographs and drawings (Deutsch and Heltzer, 1997:112) clearly show, there is no *nun* inscribed; rather, the character is most certainly a *yod* with two horizontal lines in the upper left side, one of which is hardly visible in the photograph examined by Cross.

Professor Cross' objections has been dealt with elsewhere by Professor K. McCarter Jr. (1996:40). He notes that *mšl* "ruler" was based on a misreading of the last letter as *lamed* instead of *qof*, in which case the word should be read as *mšq* "cupbearer". This new suggestion is welcomed and adopted by us (Cf. Neh. 1:11 mašqe(h)). Thus we read the inscription as *ḥṣ kty // mšq ʿbdy* "Arrow of the Kitian, cupbearer of ʿAbday".

3. A new title: *rb mkrm* is present. Therefore it is to be noted that in South-Lebanon, at the time given, a certain organization of "merchants" exist.

4. Only eight persons among the 43, which forms 19%, are of "retainers of PN", maintaining our observation about chiefs and their gangs of dependents (Deutsch and Heltzer, 1995:29–30).

5. Regarding the ethnic origin, additionally to the Egyptian *Wry* and the Cypriot Kitionian *kty* (Ibid, pp. 30–31), we find the *bn nkr* the "son of foreigner" (No.83 above). Seven persons out of 43 (17%) were not of local origin, as it is usually designated by the *niṣbe*.

6. Nine persons (18%) had the title of warriors.

7. The following names are found for the first time on arrowheads:

a) *ʾlmlk* — West-semitic (No.80 above)

b) *ʾlʿm* — West-semitic (No.82 above)

c) *ʿzr* — West-semitic (No.83 above), possibly originally *ġzr* "youth, hero", as in Ugaritic, due to the fact that here it appears in the 11th century B.C.E.

The following names are previously known from arrowheads:

d) *zkr* — West-semitic (No.84 above)

e) *mlkrm* — West-semitic (No.81 above)

8. It should be noted that the personal name ʿAbday has emerged as the most frequent name inscribed on Phoenician arrowheads. The following eight such items are listed:

1) ḥṣ kty // mšq ʿbdy "Arrow of the Kitian, cupbearer of ʿAbday" (Deutsch and Heltzer, 1994:16–18, No.4; 1997:111–112; Cross, 1995; McCarter, 1996)

2) ḥṣ ymn // ʾš ʿbdy "Arrow of Yaman, man (retainer) of ʿAbday" (Bordreuil, 1982, pp.188–192).

3) ḥṣ swr // ʾš ʿbdy "Arrow of Suwar, man (retainer) of ʿAbday" (F.M. Cross, 1996).

4) ḥṣ mlkyrm // bn ʿbdy "Arrow of Malkiram, son of ʿAbday" (Deutsch and Heltzer, 1995:17–18, No.44)

5) ḥṣ mhrn // bn ʿbdy "Arrow of Maharan, son of ʿAbday" (Ibid, p.18, No.45)

6) ḥṣ šʾ // bn ʿbdy "Arrow of Iʾ, son of ʿAbday" (Ibid, p.20, No.46)

7) ḥṣ ʿbdy // bn mlkrm "Arrow of ʿAbday, son of Malkiram" (No.81 above)

8) ḥṣ ʾlʿm // bn ʿbdy "Arrow of ʾEliʿam son of ʿAbday" (No.82 above)

Eight arrowheads (19%) bearing the name ʿAbday cannot be an accidental event. As it has been seen, ʿAbday had his *mšq* "cupbearer" (XXXII), (Deutsch and Heltzer, 1994:16–18, No.4; 1997:111–112; Cross, 1995; McCarter, 1996), as also his *ʾš* "man" (retainer). Two such retainers are recorded: *ymn* "Yaman" (XXXVII) and *swr* "Suwar" (XXXIV). He had also sons of which four are known: *1) ʾlʿm* "ʾEliʿam" (No.82 above), *2) mhrn* "Maharan" (XL), *3) mlkyrm* "Malkiram" (XXXIX), 4) *šʾ* "Šʾ" (XLI). One arrowhead bears the patronym of ʿAbday: *mlkrm* "Malkiram" (No.81 above). It seems very likely, that *ʿbdy* on all eight arrowheads is the same person. This allow us to reconstruct a part of the family tree:

mlkrm
|
ʿbdy
|
ʾlʿm *mhrn* *mlkyrm* *šʾ*

We possibly have here a first nucleus of a monarchical pre-state organization in South-Lebanon such as Abdimelek's organization (Jud, 9), with *rb ʾlf* "commander of thousands" with *rb mkrm* "chief of merchants" etc. Noteworthy are also the *ʾallufim* (pl.) chiefs of the tribes in Edom (Gen. 36:15–30, 40–43).

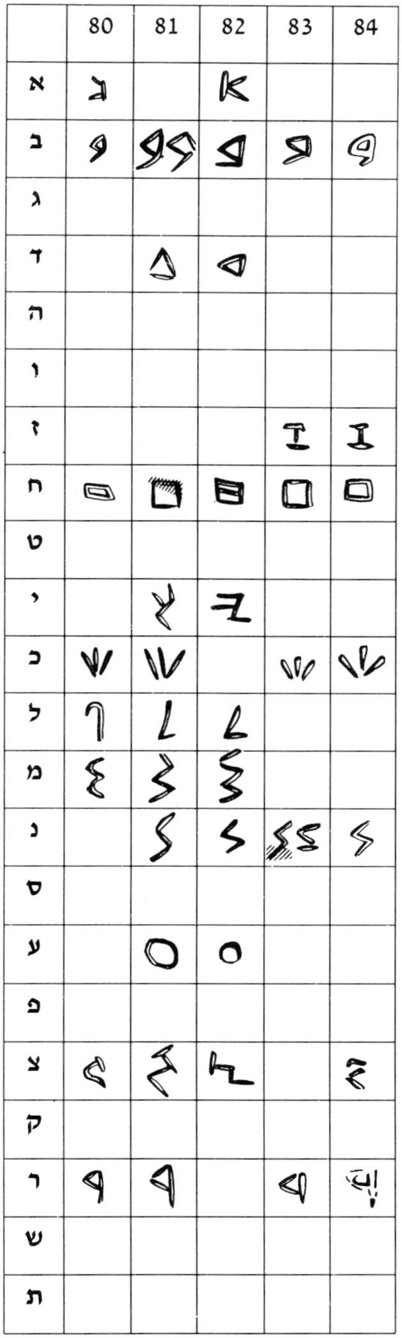

Pl. 1 Five arrowhead inscriptions

FIFTEEN HEBREW BULLAE

85.(20). **Nera᾽, son of Malkiyāhū**

Reddish-brown clay bulla, 13.2x11.7 mm. (Fig.85). The script is divided into two registers by two arched lines which terminate in papyrus flowers. The letters are carved by a skillful hand in very good calligraphic style of the second half of the 8th century B.C.E.

The easily legible inscription reads:

לנרא בן / מלכיהו

lnr᾽ bn / mlkyhw

"Belonging to Nera᾽, son of Malkīyāhū"

nr᾽ — Hypocoristicon of the Biblical name Neriyā(hū) (Jer. 32:12,16, 36:4,14 etc), with the meaning "My light is Yāhū". The name is rare and does not occur in the Bible in its shortened form. It is found incised on several handles from Gibeon *ḥnnyhw nr᾽* (Pritchard, 1959,3–6) and on seal impression on jar handles *lnr᾽ šbn᾽* (Aharoni, 1962,16–17; Deutsch and Heltzer, 1994:33–34; Vaughn, 1996:283), as also on three bullae (Deutsch, 1997, Nos.66a,b,67).

mlkyhw — The name Malkīyāhū, meaning "The God Yāhū is my king" is found in the Bible (Jer.38:6) and is very common in the Hebrew

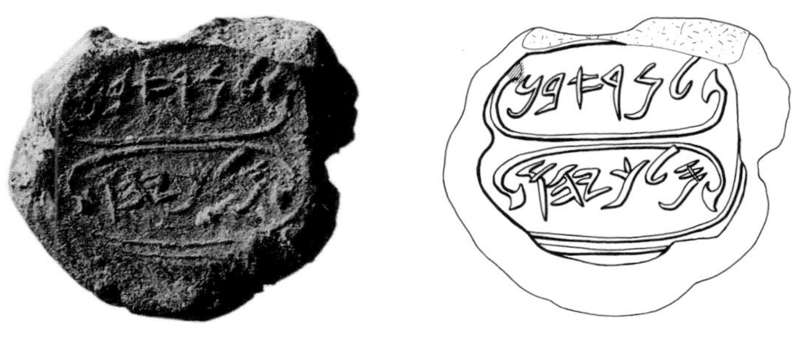

L. Wolfe collection

Fig. 85. Clay bulla belonging to "Nera᾽, son of Malkīyāhū"

epigraphy (Davies, 1991:426, 15 items listed), and on another bulla *lmlkyhw bn ywʿlyhw* (Deutsch and Heltzer, 1994:47; Deutsch, 1997, Nos.33, 59, 66a–b).

86.(21). **Neraʾ, (son of) Malkīyāhū**

Brown clay bulla, broken in two and glued, 15.0x11.9 mm. (Fig.86). The script is divided into two lines and surrounded by an elliptic double line. Around it, is decorated with a chain of pomegranates. On the back side, the papyrus impression is visible. The script is very similar to the previous one and seems that both seals which were used to seal the above bullae were made by the same hand in the second half of the 8th century B.C.E.

The inscription reads:

לנ̇רא / מלכ̇יה̇ו
lṅrʾ / mlk̇yḣw
"Belonging to Neraʾ, (son of) Malkiyāhū"

(For the names cf. above). It seems, that the seal impression which was made from another seal belonged to the same person. We have several such features, when the same person has two or more seals (Avigad, 1988:40–44; Aharoni, 1978:121, Nos.105–7; Deutsch, 1997, Nos.50a-b). Three identical bullae impressed with the same seal are kept in two private collections (Deutsch, 1997, Nos.66a-b).

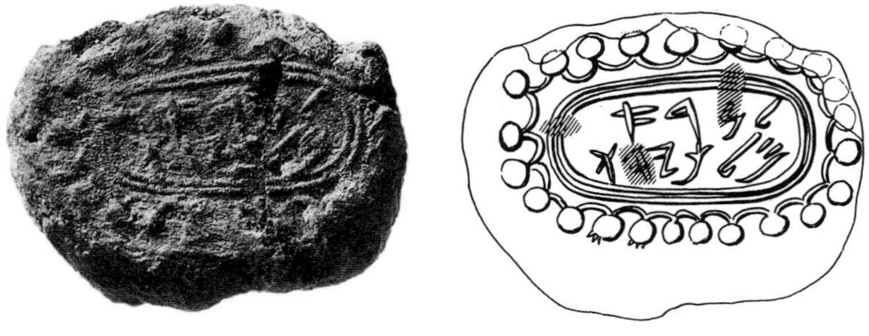

L. Wolfe collection

Fig. 86. Clay bulla belonging to "Neraʾ, (son of) Malkīyāhū"

87.(22). **Yeshaʿyāhū, (son of) Ḥilqiyāhū**

Black clay bulla, 11.8x12.2 mm. (Fig.87). On the back side, thread grooves and papyrus impressions are visible. The script is divided into two registers by a double line and surrounded by a double frame line. The script is well preserved and easily legible. It dates to the end of the 8th century B.C.E.

The inscription reads:

> **לישעיהו / חלקיהו**
> *l̇ẏšʿyhw / ḥlqyhw*
> "Belonging to Yešaʿyāhū (son of) Ḥilqiyāhū"

yšʿyhw — A frequent Biblical name *Y*^{e}*šaʿyāhū*, including the prophet Yešaʿyā (Isayah; I Chr. 3:21, 25:15, 26:25; II Reg. 19:2; Ezra 8:7,19, etc.). The name is also common in Hebrew inscriptions (Davies, 1991:381–2; Deutsch, 1997, No.88). The name appears also on bulla No.89 (Infra).

ḥlqyhw — *Ḥilqiyāhū*, meaning "My share is (the god) Yāhū". Biblical name (Jer. 1:1; II Reg. 18:37, 22:8; Neh. 8:4, 12:5 etc.). Very common name in Hebrew inscriptions (Davies, 1991:352; Deutsch, 1997, Nos.2, 30).

L. Wolfe collection

Fig. 87. Clay bulla belonging to "Yešaʿyāhū (son of) Hilqiyāhū"

88.(23) Rāfaʾyāhū, (son of) Mattanyāhū

Light brown clay bulla, 16.3x15.5 mm. (Fig.88). On the back side, thread grooves and papyrus impressions are visible. The surface is divided into three registers. In the upper register, a four winged snake *Uraeus* is depicted. The script is divided into the two lower registers all surrounded by a frame line. The script is poorly preserved but it is of very good calligraphic style of the second half of the 8th century B.C.E. and is easily legible.

The inscription reads:

[ל]רפאיהו / [מ]תניהו
[l]rpʾyhw / [m]tnyhw
"[Belonging to] Rāfaʾyāhū (son of) [Ma]ttanyāhū"

This inscription appears on another, uniconic bulla, possibly belonging to the same person (Deutsch and Heltzer, 1995:53, No.58).

rpʾyhw — lit. "(The god) Yāhū is my health/healer". The name is known from the OT in its shortened forms *Rāfāʾ* (I Chr.4:12; 8:2) and *R^{e}fāyā* (Neh.3:9; I Chr.3:21; 4:42 etc.), as also the form *R^{e}fāʾēl* (I Chr.26:7). The name appears on other four Hebrew bullae: 1) *lrfʾyhw / bn ʾfrḥ* "Belonging to Rāfayāhū, son of ʾEfraḥ" (Shoham, 1994, No.17) 2) *lmšlm [b/n] rfʾyhw* "Belonging to Mešullam so[n of] Rāfayāhū" 3) *ln[ḥ]m bn / rfʾ[yhw]* "Belonging to Na[ḥ]um son of Rāfa[yāhū]" (Avigad,

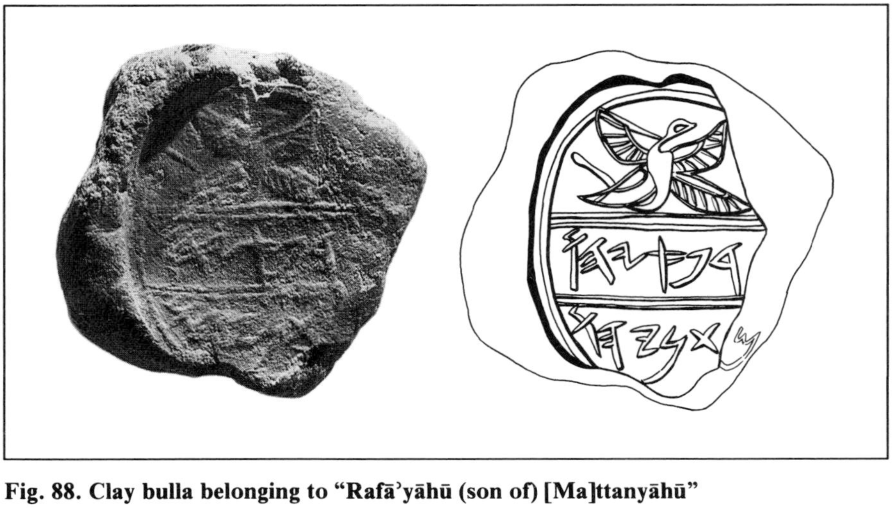

Fig. 88. Clay bulla belonging to "Rafāʾyāhū (son of) [Ma]ttanyāhū"

1988, Nos.111, 121) 4) *lšfn* / *rfʾyhw* "Belonging to Šafan (son of) Rāfayāhū" (Deutsch, 1997, No.94).

mtnyhw — One of the most common Hebrew names meaning "Gift of (the God) Yāhū". The name is known from the OT (II Reg.24:17; Ezra10:26, Neh.12:25 etc.) and is listed ten times by Davies (1991:436–7). It appears also on three recently published bullae (Deutsch, 1997, Nos.20, 62, 63).

89.(24). **Ṣaphan, son of Y^{i}/ešaʿyāhū**

Reddish-brown clay bulla, 11.2x12.5 mm. (Fig.89). On the back side, thread grooves and papyrus impressions are visible. The seal surface is divided into three registers by two double lines. In the upper register, a two-winged snake *Uraeus* is depicted. The script is divided into the two lower registers. The script is of the end of the 8th century B.C.E. and is easily legible.

The inscription reads:

לצפן בן / ישׂעיהו
lṣpn bn / yš̊ʿyhẇ
"Belonging to Ṣafan, son of Yešaʿyāhū"

ṣpn — Hypocoristicon of the Biblical name *ṣpnyhw* meaning "God has hidden, treasured" (I Chr.6:21; Jer.21:1 etc.). The name *ṣpnyhw* and its hypocoristicon *ṣpn* appears frequently in the Hebrew epigraphy and was listed 23 times by Davies (1991:477–8), twice by Deutsch and Heltzer (1995, Nos.52, 55) and three times by Deutsch (1997, Nos.83, 84, 90).

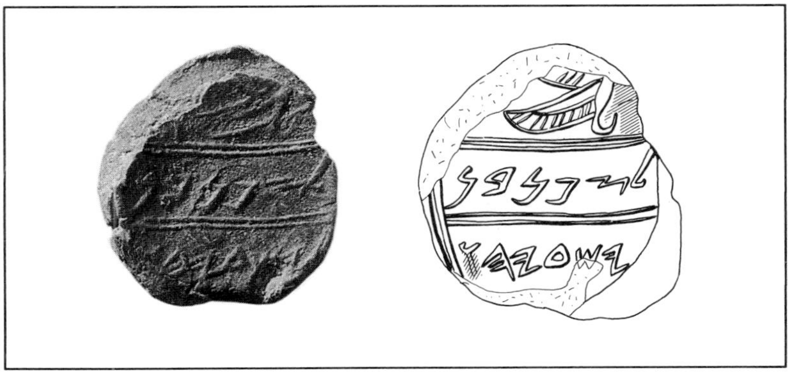

Fig. 89. Clay bulla belonging to "Ṣafan, son of Yešaʿyāhū"

yšʿyhw — A frequent Biblical name *Yᵉšaʿyāhū*, including the prophet Yešaʿyā (I Chr. 3:21, 25:15, 26:25; II Reg. 19:2; Ezra 8:7,19, etc.). The name is also common in Hebrew inscriptions (Davies, 1991:38; Deutsch, 1997, No.88). The name appears also on bulla No.87 (Supra).

90.(25). *Yhʾr*, son of Hošaʿyāhū

A broken brown clay bulla, 15.8x11.4 mm. (Fig.90). On the back side, thread grooves are visible. The seal surface is divided into two registers by a double line and surrounded by a frame line. The script is of the 7th century B.C.E. The lower part of the bulla is missing but is easily restored and legible.

The inscription reads:

ליהאר / [ב]ן הושעיהו
lyhʾr / [b]ṅ ḣẇšʿẏhw
"Belonging to Yehoʾur, son of Hošaʿayāhū"

yhʾr — A previously unrecorded theophoric name meaning "(The God) Yāh is the light". The theophoric element is written in an abridged manner — yh at the beginning of the name. The parallels *Ūriʾēl*, *Ūriyāh* and *Ūriyāhū* are known from the OT (I Chr. 6:9, II Chr.13:2; II Sam.11:3,7,8; Jer.26:20,21,23 etc.). Another parallel is the name *ʾlyʾr* which appears in Hebrew and Ammonite epigraphy, on an ostraca from Arad (Aharoni, 1978, 21:2), on the seal *ʾlʾr* (Aufrecht, 1989, Nos.134 and 148) etc. Another Ammonite parallel is the name Milkomʾūr found on the official bulla *lmlkmʾwr / ʿb/d bʿlyšʿ* "Belonging to Milkomʾūr servant

L. Wolfe collection

Fig. 90. Clay bulla belonging to "Yahuʾur, son of Hošaʿayāhū"

of Baʿalyišʿ" (Geraty, 1985:98–9; Herr, 1985)

hwšʿyhw — lit. "(The God) Yāhū saved" is known from the OT as Hošaʿāyā and Hošeʿa (Jer.42:1, 43:2; Neh.12:32 etc.). The name Hošaʿayahu is very common in the Hebrew epigraphy and is listed 22 times by Davies (1991:334) and twice on bullae by Deutsch (1997, Nos.41–2). The name Hošeʿa appears also twice on bulla No.96 (Infra).

91.(26). ʾUšnāʾ

A gray clay bulla, 10.5x15.5 mm. (Fig.91). The script is divided into two registers by a single line and surrounded by a frame line. The script of the end of the 7th century or early 6th century B.C.E. was carelessly executed. It seems as it was a bone seal which was used to impress this bulla. Only the seal owners name appears omitting the name of his father.

The inscription reads:

לאש/נא
lʾš/nʾ
"Belonging to ʾŪšnāʾ"

ʾšnʾ — The name is rare and it is missing in the OT. It is probably a shortened form of a theophoric name such as **ʾšnyhw* with the root *ʾwš* "to give (strength)" (Fowler, 1988:335), meaning "May Yahwe give" (Avigad, 1979:121). The name appears on the Israelite royal official seal *lʾšnʾ ʿ/bd ʾḥz* "Belonging to ʾŪšnāʾ, servant of Aḥaz" (Torrey, 1940;

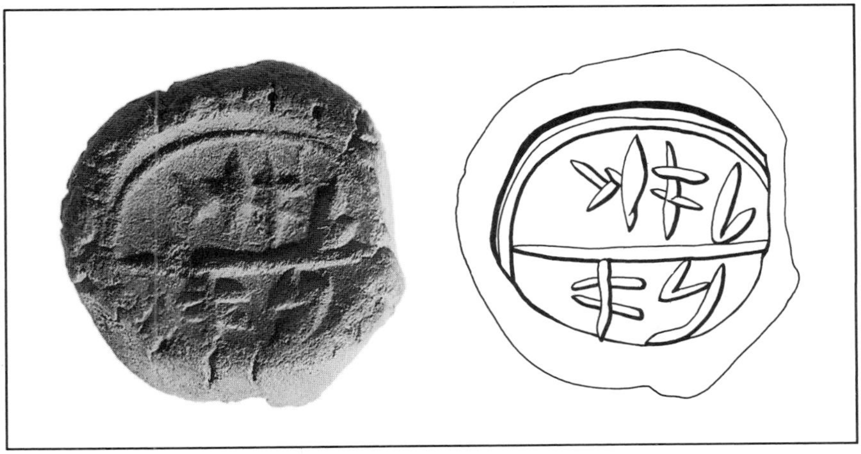

Fig. 91. Clay bulla belonging to "ʾŪšnāʾ"

Bordreuil, 1985, No.23) and on the Judean seals *lkslʾ* / *ʾšnʾ* "Belonging to Kislaʾ, (son of) ʾŪšnāʾ" (Deutsch and Heltzer, 1994:60, No.27), *lʾšnʾ* "Belonging to ʾŪšnāʾ" (Hestrin and Dayagi, 1979:64, No.40) and *[lʾ]šnʾ* "[Belonging to ʾŪ]šnāʾ" (Avigad, 1979, No.2). This is for the first time that this name occurs on a bulla.

92.(27). **Baqqeš, son of Benayāhū**

A brown clay bulla, 16.5x15.5 mm. (Fig.92). The script is divided into two registers by a double line and surrounded by a double frame line. The script belongs to the first half of the 7th century B.C.E.

The inscription reads:

[ל]בקש ב/[ן] בֿניהו
[l]bqš b/[n] ḃnyhw
"Belonging to Bqš, son of Benayāhū"

An identical bulla sealed with the same seal was recently published (Deutsch, 1997, No.40).

bqš — An hypocoristicon, unknown from the OT. The root *bqš* means "To ask, to demand". In our case we possibly have *Baqquš* (Part. pass piʿel) "The demanded, the pleaded (from God)". The name is rare and appears on the seal: *lsmk (son of) bqš* "Belonging to Samakh, (son of) Baqqesh" (Hestrin and Dayagi, 1979:107, No.83) and on an Ammonite seal *lbqš bn ndbʾl* "Belonging to Baqqesh, son of Nadabʾēl" (ibid:130, No.103).

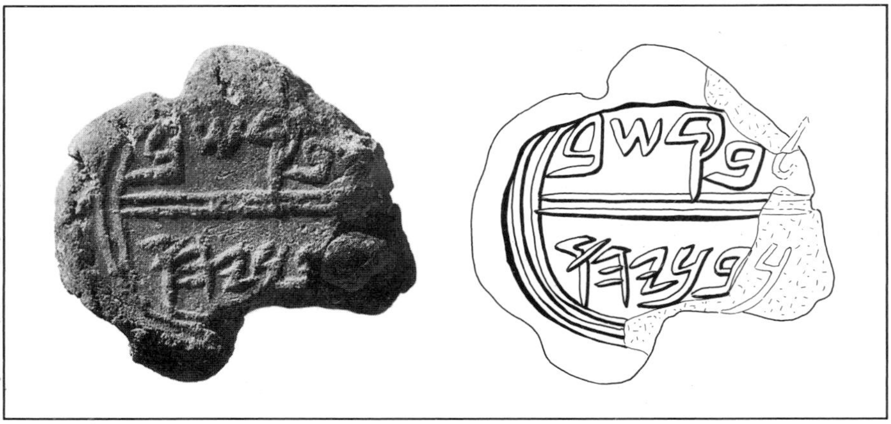

Fig. 92. Clay bulla belonging to "Bqš, son of Benayāhū"

bnyhw — Biblical name (II Sam.23:22; I Reg.1:8; I Chr.11:31; II Chr.31:13 etc.) meaning "(The God) Yāhū created, erected". Common name in the Hebrew epigraphic sources, listed nine times by Davies (1991:315), twice by Deutsch (1997, Nos.39,40) and twice by Deutsch and Heltzer (1995, Nos.60,79:18).

93a-b.(28). **ʾElišamaʿ, son of ʾEfraḥ**

Two identical light brown clay bullae, sealed by the same seal. Both partly damaged. **a.** 16.0x13.0 mm. (Fig.93a) **b.** 12.0x12.0 mm. (Fig.93b). The script is divided into two registers by a double line. The letters are carelessly executed and are to be dated to the second half of the 7th century B.C.E.

The inscription reads:

a. **לאלשמ[ע] / בֹּן אפרח**
lʾlšm[ʿ] / bn ʾfrḥ

b. **[ל]אלשמ[ע / ב]ן אפר[ח]**
[l]ʾlšm[ʿ / b]n ʾfr[ḥ]
"Belonging to ʾElišamaʿ, son of ʾEfraḥ"

ʾlšmʿ — The name ʾElišamaʿ meaning "My God listened" is common in the OT in its full spelling "ʾElyšāmaʿ" (I Chr.2:41; II Chr.17:7–8; II Reg.25:25 etc.). The name is very common in the Hebrew epigraphic sources and is listed 16 times by Davies (1991:284–5), twice by Deutsch (1997, Nos.33,34) and twice by Deutsch and Heltzer (1994:46, 1995:59).

Fig. 93. Clay bullae belonging to "ʾElišamaʿ, son of ʾEfraḥ"

ʾprḥ — The name ʾEfraḥ means "to flourish" (Heltzer and Ohana, 1978:35), rather than "chick" (Avigad, 1988:35, No.19). This name is missing in the OT but its very common in the Hebrew epigraphic sources which is listed 10 times by Davies (1991:289) and once by Deutsch (1997, No.36).

94a-c.(29). **ʾAḥiqam, son of Ḥaby**

Three identical brown clay bullae, sealed by the same seal. (All three partly broken. **a.** 15.8x18.8 mm. (Fig.94a) **b.** 24.0x21.5 mm. (Fig.94b) **c.** 17.0x15.2 mm. (Fig.94c). The script is divided into two registers by a "lotus bud design" and surrounded by a framing line. The letters are carved by a skillful hand in very good calligraphic style of the second half of the 8th century B.C.E.

The inscription reads:

a. **לאחיק[ם] / בן ח[בי]**
lʾḥyq[m] / bn ḥ[by]
b. **[לאח]יקם / בן חבי**
[lʾḥ]yqm / bn ḥby
c. **[לאחיקם] / בן חבי**
[lʾḥyqm] / bn ḥby
"Belonging to ʾAḥiqam, son of Ḥaby (or Ḥabay)"

Seven identical fragmentary bullae are on display at the Hecht Museum in Haifa (AHL, in print).

ʾḥyqm — Biblical name meaning "My (divine) brother arises". In the OT Aḥiqam son of Šafan was a high official in the days of King Josiah (II Reg.22:12,14). The name appears in the Hebrew epigraphic sources and was listed three times by Davies (1991:274) and twice by Deutsch (1997, Nos.24,25, including one of Aḥiqam son of Šafan). It is also recorded in its shortened form *ʾḥqm*, six times by Davies (ibid, p.275) and once by Deutsch and Heltzer, 1995:92 79:8).

ḥby — "Ḥaby or Ḥabay" Theophoric hypocoristicon known from the OT in its more complete form *ḥbyh* "Ḥabyāh" (Ezra 2:61; Neh. 7:63). Avigad (1988, No.52) published a bulla: *lḥbʾ b/n mtn* "Belonging to *Ḥbʾ*, son of Mattan". He argues that the root is *ḥbʾ* "to hide, to make confidently". The full theophoric name with the root *ḥbʾ* is *ʾElyaḥbaʾ* (II Sam.23:32; I Chr.11:33). See also the name *Yeḥubba* (I Chr.7:34). The full name as Avigad points out (1988:49) had to be *Ḥabayāhū*. The name appears also in a seal impression on jar handle *ḥby / ḥgy* "(Belonging to) Ḥaby, (son of) Ḥaggay" (Infra No. 115).

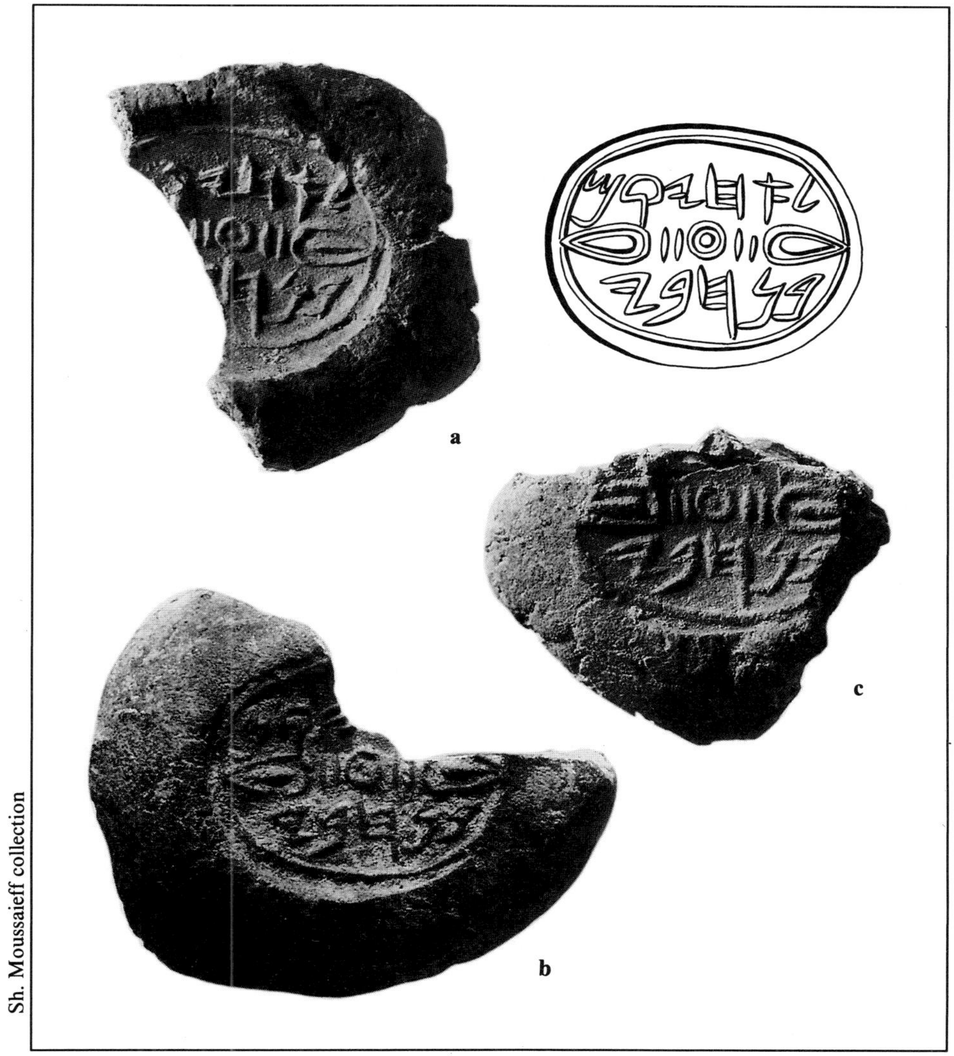

Fig. 94. Clay bullae belonging to "ʾAḥiqam, son of Ḥaby"

L. Wolfe collection

Fig. 95. Clay bulla belonging to "*Blbl*, [son of ...]"

95.(30). *Blbl*, (son of ...)

The upper part of a brown clay bulla, 17.5x14.5 mm. (Fig.95). On the back of the bulla the impression of textile has survived. The letters are carelessly executed. The three letters *l* (lamed) are angular and differ one of each other. A date to the second half of the 7th century B.C.E. is to be preferred. The name of the owner is clear but the name of his father is lost.

The inscription reads:

> **לבלבל / ...**
> *lblbl* / ...
> "Belonging to *Blbl*, [son of ...]"

blbl — The name is rare and appears only once on an Edomite ostracon from Horvat ʿUzza (Beit-Arieh and Cresson, 1985:96 1:1). The etymology as also the vocalization are not clear. An example of a similar derivation is to be found on the bulla: *lyhwʾ* / *bn* / *mšmš* "Belonging to Yehū, son of *Mšmš*" (Avigad, 1988, No.70). The name may have be given after the Arabic bird name *Bulbul* (Beit-Arieh and Cresson, 1985:97).

96.(31). Hōšeaʿ, (son of) ʾAkhbor, (son of) ʾElišāmaʿ, (son of) Hōšeaʿ

Light brown clay bulla, broken and glued. Its size is 18.0x22.5 mm., and the impression size is 12.5x13.3 mm. (Fig.96). On its edge are fingerprints and on the back of the bulla impression of papyrus has survived. The inscription has been divided into four registers by three lines and surrounded by a circular line. The letters are angular and carelessly executed. A date around 600 B.C.E. is to be considered.

The inscription reads:

להושע / עכבר אל/שמע הׄוׄ/שע |

lhwšᶜ | ᶜkbr ʾl̄/šmᶜ hw̄/šᶜ |

"Belonging to Hōšeaᶜ, (son of) ᶜAkhbor, (son of) ʾElišāmaᶜ, (son of) Hōšeaᶜ"

The legend contains the seal owners name, his fathers, his grand fathers and his grand grand fathers names. This is for the first time that we find a seal mentioning four generations. We also observe the paponym phenomenon where the seal owner has been named after his grand grand fathers name, which was probably a prominent person.

hwšᶜ — Hōšeaᶜ, hypocoristicon of the name Hošaᶜyāhū. Common Biblical name (I Chr.27:20; II Reg.15:30; the book of Hōšeaᶜ, etc.), recorded seven times in the Hebrew epigraphy (Davies, 1991:333) and 24 times in its full form: Hošaᶜyāhū (ibid, p.334; Deutsch, 1997, Nos.41,42).

ᶜkbr — lit. "mouse", Biblical ᶜAkhbor (I Chr.1:49; II Reg.22:12,14;

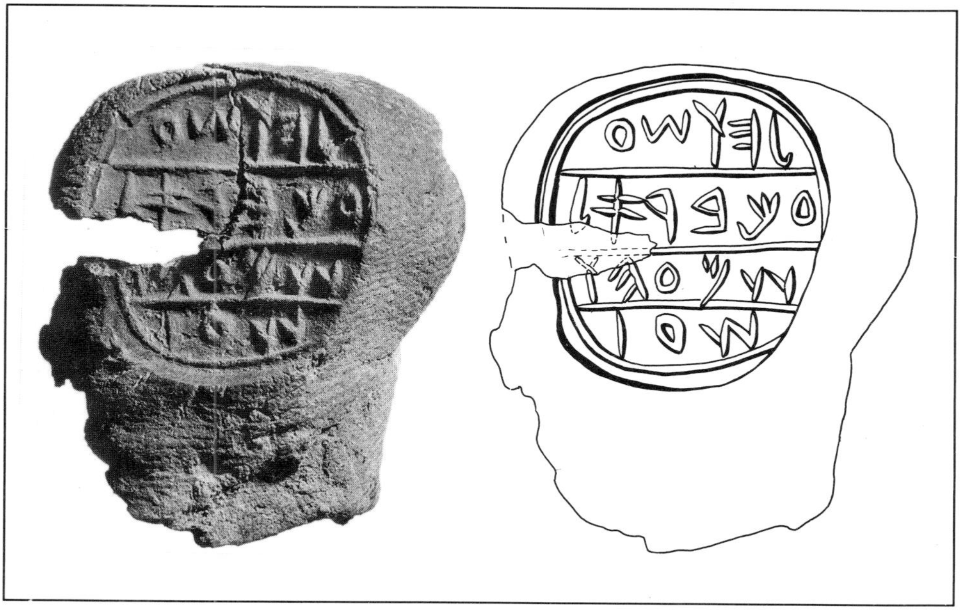

Fig. 96. Clay bulla belonging to "Hōšeaᶜ, (son of) ᶜAkhbor, (son of) ʾElišāmaᶜ, (son of) Hōšeaᶜ"

Jer.26:22 etc.). Common name in the Hebrew epigraphy, recorded three times by Davies (1991:460), twice by Deutsch and Heltzer (1995, Nos.55,79:11) and three times by Deutsch (1997, Nos.76a-c). The name appears also frequently in Punic (Benz, 1972:171).

ʾlšmʿ — ʾElišāmaʿ "My god heard". The name is widely dispersed in the OT in its full spelling ʾEliyšāmaʿ (II Chr.17:7–9; II Reg.25:25 etc.), as also in the Hebrew epigraphic sources (Davies, 1991:284–5, recorded 16 times; Deutsch and Heltzer, 1994, No.19; 1995, No.62; Deutsch, 1997, Nos.33,34).

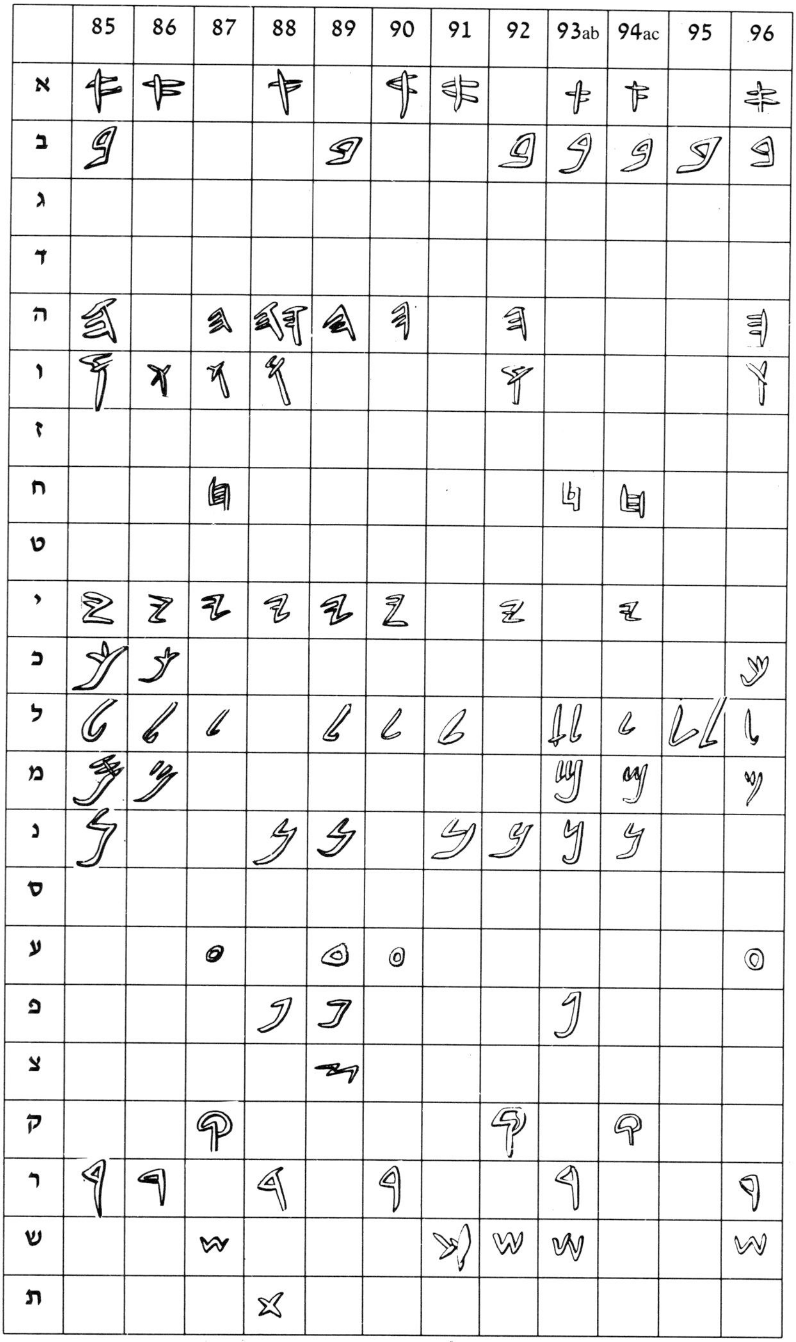

Pl. 2 Fifteen Hebrew seal impression inscriptions

FIFTEEN WEST SEMITIC SEALS

Four Israelite Hebrew Seals

97.(20) **Silver signet ring of Noiyāw**

The seal is made of silver and it was cast in the "lost wax" technique. It is 20.6 mm. in diameter and its seal is 10.9x14.9x4.2 mm. in size. The ring terminates in two papyrus flowers. The surface of the seal is divided into three registers by two double lines and is surrounded by an 1 mm. thick eminent frame. In the upper register a falcon with eagle spread wings is depicted and in the lower register a two winged scarab is carved.

The inscription reads:

> **לנויו**
> *lnwyw*
> "Belonging to Nōiyāw (Noiyō)"

The letter *y* (*yod*) has a cursive tail. The two letters *w* (waw) are slightly different but both are typical Northern Israeli and are to be dated to the VIII century B.C.E.

nwyw — Private name with the theophoric yahwistic element *yw*, characteristic to the Northern kingdom dialect. The name is not found in the OT and formerly unknown from other epigraphic sources.

A possible etymology with the root *n'h* "to ornate" is to be considered. Cf. Cant. 1:10 *na'wu l*^{e}*ḥāyayik* "Your cheeks got pretty"; 2:14 *umar*$^{e'}$*ek nā'weh* "and your looking is pretty". Later, in the post-exilic Hebrew, the same word "prettiness" is *nwy* — *nōy*. Therefore, a possible meaning of the name will be "My prettiness (grace) is Yāū".

Sh. Moussaieff collection

Fig. 97. Israelite silver signet ring belonging to "Nōiyaw (Noiyō)"

98.(21). **The seal of Domlā᾽, son of Peqaḥyāū (Peqaḥyō)**

Lapis-Lazuli dome shaped unperforated scaraboid seal. It is 16.0x12.1x6.1 mm. in size. The surface of the seal is divided into two registers by a single line. In the upper register the bust of the Egyptian lioness-headed goddess Sekhmet is depicted, similar to the one which appears on the seal of "᾽Asafyāū" (Deutsch and Heltzer, 1995:59–60). In the lower register, a two line inscription is engraved.

The inscription reads:

לדמלא ב/ן פקחיו
ldml᾽ b/n pqḥyw
"Belonging to Domlā᾽, son of Peqaḥyāū (Peqaḥyō)"

dml᾽ — The name does not appear in the OT, but is known from epigraphic sources. It appears on a clay bulla (Avigad, 1975:70, No.18), five times in the Gibeon inscriptions (Pritchard, 1959:21) and on a sherd from Samaria-Sebaste (Crowfoot, J.W. et al., 1957:21). The non-hypocoristic names *dml᾽l* is found on the seal *lqlyhw / dml᾽l* (Horn, 1968). Here the name is possibly a hypocoristicon of **dmlyw* (Fowler, 1988:165). The name *dmlyhw* is common and is recorded 11 times (Davies, 1991:331).

pqḥyw — possibly vocalized *Paqaḥyāū, means "Yau has opened (the eyes or ears)". The shortened name "Peqaḥ" is known and common in the OT (II Reg. 15:16; Jer. 7:1; II Chr. 28:6) as also Peqaḥyā(h) (II Reg.

Fig. 98 Israelite lapis-lazuli seal belonging to "Domlā᾽, son of Peqaḥyāū (Peqaḥyō)"

15:22,26). The shortened name *pqḥ* appears on an ostracon from Lachish (Lachish III:338), on a jar sherd from Hazor *lpqḥ smdr* (or *smry*) (Hazor II:69, Pl. CLXXI), on a seal from Nablus *pqḥ* (Bordreuil, 1986a) and on two Hebrew bullae, one of a woman ... / *bt pqḥ* and the second of a man *lbnyhw* / *bn nryhw* / *bn pqḥ* (Deutsch, 1997, Nos.17,39). As also, the name *pqḥy* appears on the seal from Jericho *ʾḥyw pqḥy* (Sachau, 1896).

Sh. Moussaieff collection

Fig. 99. Israelite steatite scarab seal belonging to "Saʿadyāū (Saʿadyō)"

99.(22). **The seal of Saʿadyāū (Saʿadyō)**

White steatite scarab seal, 19.1x13.4x18.5 mm. in size, and lengthwise perforated. The field is divided into three registers by two lines and surrounded by a border line. The larger upper register depicts a winged griffin standing to left, wearing kilt and the Royal double crown of the upper and lower Egypt. Before him appears an *ankh*, the Egyptian "Key of life" symbol. The inscription is engraved in the middle register and a wavy line in the lower one.

The Inscription reads:

[ל]סעדיו
[l]sʿdyw
"Belonging to Saʿadyāū (Saʿadyō)"

The shape of the letter *w* (waw), the iconography as also the name are typical Northern Israeli of the VIII century B.C.E.

sʿdyw — Rare theophoric name meaning "My help is Yāhū" as in verse "יהוה יסעדני", (Ps. 94:18). The south, i.e. Judean parallel *sʿdyhw* and its shortened forms *sʿdh*, *sʿdyh* are also scarce (Davies, 1991:449; Deutsch, 1997, No.70).

Addenda
to the Israelite seals

Our corpus of Israelite seals is scarce today and these presented here are an important addition to it. With no doubt, the corpus of Israelite seals from the northern kingdom is steadily growing including the seal of Asafyāū (Deutsch and Heltzer, 1995, No.63) and the inscribed seal-mould (ibid. No.75). This contribution widens our knowledge about Israeli glyptics and epigraphy and it will bring us to separate the treating of Judean and Israelite epigraphy in general and seals in particular.

R. Deutsch M. Heltzer

Six Judean Seals

100.(23). **The seal of Nerāʾ (son of) Meyšar**

Red carnelian dome shaped scaraboid seal, 15.1x11.8x7.2 mm. in size and unperforated. The field is divided into two registers by a single line and surrounded by a border line. The larger upper register depicts a winged griffin standing to right, wearing kilt and the Royal double crown of the Upper and Lower Egypt. Before him appears the *ankh* sign, which is the Egyptian symbol "Key of life". The inscription is engraved in two lines in the lower register.

The inscription reads:

> **לנרא / מישר**
> *lnrʾ / myšr*
> "Belonging to Nerāʾ (son of) Meyšar"

The name Nerāʿ is a hypocoristicon of the Biblical name Neriyāhū (Jer. 36:14), meaning "The God (Yāhū) is my light", widely known in the Hebrew epigraphy, recorded 19 times by Davies (1991:443–4) once by Deutsch and Heltzer (1994, No.9) and three times by Deutsch (1997, Nos.66a-b, 67).

The name *Myšr* appears for the first time in the west semitic inscriptions and is unknown from the OT (Unrecorded by Zadok, 1988). The meaning of the root yšr is "to be straight, to be righteous". In Hebrew we have the

Sh. Moussaieff collection

Fig. 100. Judean carnelian seal belonging to "Nerāʾ (son of) Meyšar"

word *meyšarīm* "uprightness, fairness" and from here "equity". Cf. Prov. 1:3 *ṣedeq umišpaṭ u mēšārīm* "righteousness, justice and equity". We have to note that these terms, substitute one another. In Punic the term *myšr* means "justice" (KAI, 161,2) (Part., Piᶜel). Μιςωρ appears together with Συδυκ in the fragments of Philo of Byblos, speaking about righteousness and equity, as also in a number of Phoenician inscriptions such as the IV century B.C.E. Yeḥawmilk stele (KAI 104), as a "king of righteousness and equity" 6) ...*mlk ṣdq umlk* 7) *yšr* (Liverani, 1971; Lipinski, 1995:112–4). In Babylonia the term *mešārum* had the meaning of the abolishment of debts and even the release of debt-slaves (Kraus, 1984). Therefore, a possible etymology of the name *myšr* is "The man of righteousness, equity".

101.(24). **The seal of Ḥilleṣyāhū, son of (the) king**

Blue Lapis lazuli stone scaraboid seal, lengthwise perforated and 15.6x13.5x8.5 mm. in size. The field is divided into two registers by a double line and surrounded by a double border line. The larger upper register depicts a winged crouching sphinx. Before him appears the sign *ankh*, the Egyptian "Key of life" symbol. The name of the seal owner and his title are engraved around the sphinx and in the lower register.

The Hebrew inscription reads:

לחלצ/י/הו / בן מלך

lḥlṣ/y/hw // bn mlk

"Belonging to Ḥilleṣyāhū, son of (the) king"

Fig. 101. Judean lapis-lazuli seal belonging to "Ḥilleṣyāhū, son of (the) king"

The sphinx is a common motif in the Phoenician iconography. Here, a Phoenician seal has been chosen and the Hebrew name was added by a Hebrew owner. The paleography and the iconography point toward a date in the second half of the VIII Century B.C.E.

ḥlṣyhw — Theophoric name derived from the root *ḥlṣ* of the Piʿel stem meaning "to save, to rescue". The name is missing from the OT but is recorded six times in the Hebrew epigraphy:

1) *lḥlṣyhw? ...* "Belonging to Ḥilleṣyāhū? ..." (Lemaire, 1986, No.4)
2) *lmlkyhw (bn) ḥlṣyhw* "Belonging to Malkiyāhū (son of) Ḥilleṣyāhū" (Reifenberg, 1954:140)
3) *lʾlšmʿ (bn) ḥlṣyhw* "Belonging to ʾElišamaʿ (son of) Ḥilleṣyāhū" (Lemaire, 1985, No.6)
4) *lhwšʿyhw (bn) ḥlṣyhw* "Belonging to Hošaʿyāhū son of Ḥilleṣyāhū" (Avigad, 1986, No.46)
5) *lyšmʿʾl bn šʿl (bn) ḥlṣyhw* "Belonging to Yišmaʿʾel, son of Šuaʿl (son of) Ḥilleṣyāhū" (Avigad, 1986, No.79)
6) *lrʾyhw (bn) ḥlṣyhw* "Belonging to Rāʾayāhū (son of) Ḥilleṣyāhū" Avigad, 1986, No.157)

bn mlk "son of (the) king, prince". The article *h* (he) is missing. The same phenomenon appears in the bulla *lntn ʾšr ʿl byt* "Belonging to Natan who is over (the) house" (Avigad, 1986, No.3). The name of the king is not mentioned. The above presented prince seal rise the number of seals belonging to "sons of the king" of Judah to 17:

1. *ʾlšmʿ* "ʾElšmaʿ" (Vattioni, 1969, No.72; Barkay, 1993, No.2)
2. *gʾlyhw* "Geʾalyāhū" (Beth-Zur, Sellers, 1933:60–1; Barkay, 1993, No.3)
3. *gʾlyhw* "Geʾalyāhū" (Avigad, 1986, No.6; Barkay, 1993, No.4)
4. *gdyhw* "Gaddiyāhū" (Bordreuil and Lemaire, 1979:71–2, No.1 Barkay, 1993, No.5)
5. *hllyhw* "Hillelyāhū" (DHL, A44; Barkay, 1993, No.1 sic.)
6. *yhwʾḥz* "Yehoʾaḥaz" (Hestrin and Dayagi, 1979, No.6; Barkay, 1993, No.6)
7. *yrḥmʾl* "Yeraḥmeʾēl" (Avigad, 1986, No.8; Barkay, 1993, No.7)
8. *yšmʿʾl* "Yišmaʿēl" (Barkay, 1993; and No.17)
9. *mlkyhw* "Malkiyāhū" (NFA, 1991, No.50; Barkay, 1993, No.16)

10. *mnšh* "Menaše" (Avigad, 1987a:201–203; Barkay, 1993, No.9. There is another seal of *mnšh bn hmlk* which is not Hebrew but probably Moabite (Vattioni, 1969, No.209; Barkay, 1993, No.8)
11. *nryhw* "Neriyāhū" (Avigad, 1986, No.7; Barkay, 1993, No.11)
12. *nryhw* "Neriyāhū" (Avigad, 1988:41–2; Barkay, 1993, No.10)
13. *nryhw* "Neriyāhū" (Avigad, 1988:41–2; Barkay, 1993, No.12)
14. *pdyhw* "Padayāhū" (Avigad, 1992; Barkay, 1993, No.13)
15. *šbnyhw* "Šebanayāhū" (Avigad, 1981:304; Barkay, 1993, No.15)
16. *šbnyhw* "Šebanayāhū" (Aharoni, 1968:166; Barkay, 1993, No.14)

Two princesses are also recorded"

17. *mᶜdnh* "Maᶜadanā" (Avigad, 1978; Barkay, 1993, No.18)
18. *nwyh* "Nōiyā" (Deutsch, 1997, No.14)

About the status and the functions of "the king's sons" see (Lemaire, 1979:197–9; Avigad, 1986:27–8; Barkay, 1993:110–12; Avishur and Heltzer, 1996:46–54).

102.(25). **The seal of Ḥāšabyāhū son of Šāfaṭyāhū**

White agate stone scaraboid seal, lengthwise perforated and 13.2x9.9x 7.6 mm. in size. The field is divided into two registers by a double line and surrounded by a double border line.

The Hebrew inscription reads:

לחשביהו ב/ן שפטיהו
lḥšbyhw b/n špṭyhw
"Belonging to Ḥāšabyāhū son of Šhāfaṭyāhū"

A. Saeedi collection

Fig. 102. Judean agate seal belonging to "Ḥašabyāhū son of Šhāfaṭyāhū"

On the paleographical ground, square *l* (lamed) and the shape of the letter w (waw), the seal is to be dated to the 7th century B.C.E..

ḥšbyhw — Theophoric private name meaning "Yāhū has decided, planned", common in the OT (I Chr. 6:30, 25:3, 26:30; Ezra 8:19; Neh. 11:15 etc.).

špṭyhw — Common Biblical name known as *Šefaṭyāhū*, *Šᵉfaṭyā(h)* (II Sam. 3:4; Jer. 38:1; I Chr. 3:3, 9:8 etc.), meaning "Yāhū has judged". The name is also common in the Hebrew epigraphy, recorded ten times by Davies (1991:504) and once by Deutsch (1997, No. 69).

103.(26). **The seal of Gemalyāhū, son of Mattān**

Bronze seal, 14.5x12.4x5.9 mm. in size, lengthwise perforated. The field is divided into two registers by a double line and surrounded by a single border line. The other side is decorated with a gazelle? surrounded by dots.

The 7th century B.C.E. Hebrew inscription reads:

לגׄמליהׄו / בן מתן

lġmlyhẇ / bn mtn

"Belonging to Gemalyāhū, son of Mattan"

gmlyhw — The etymology has to be "Yāhū compensates, renders". Only the hypocoristicon *Gᵉmalī* appears in the OT (Nu. 13:12) as a *hapax legomenon* and the parallel *Gamlīʾēl* (Nu. 1:10, 2:20 etc.). The name appears on an 8th century B.C.E. jug inscription (Lemaire, 1982) and on four seals: 1) *lgmlyhw* "Belonging to Gemalyāhū" (AHL, No.24), 2) *lgmlyhw (bn) ʾdnyḥy* "Belonging to Gemalyāhū (son) of ʾAdōnyḥay" (AHL, No.25), 3) *ldlyhw bn gmlyhw* "Belonging to Delyāhū son of Gemalyāhū" (AHL, No.5), 4) *lḥṣy bn gmlyhw* "Belonging to *Ḥṣy* son of Gemalyāhū" (Avigad, 1954:149–150).

mtn — Hypocoristicon of the Biblical name Mattanyāhū meaning "gift of Yāhū" (II Reg. 11:18; II Chr. 23:17; Jer. 38:1). The name *mtn* is very common on Hebrew seals and bullae. It is recorded 18 times by Davies (1991:436) and twice by Deutsch (1997, Nos. 15a,b).

Sh. Moussaieff collection

Fig. 103. Judean bronze seal belonging to "Gemalyāhū, son of Mattan"

104.(27). **The seal of Miqneyāhū**

Bone stamp seal, oval with a perforated handle, 16.0x10.5x15.5 mm. in size. Its surface is surrounded by a framing line.

The 7th century B.C.E. Hebrew inscription reads:

מקניהו
mknyhw
"(Belonging to) Miqneyāhū"

mqnyhw — Theophoric name meaning "The property of Yāhū". The name Miqneyāhū occurs only once in the OT and belonged to a gatekeeper in the time of King David (I Chr. 15:18). In the Hebrew epigraphy the name appears five times, on an ostraca from Arad (Aharoni, 1978, 60:4), on two seals: *lmqnyhw (bn) ʾḥmlk* "Belonging to Miqneyāhū (son of) ʾAḥimelek" (AHL, No.50) *lmqnyhw bn yhwkl* "Belonging to Miqneyāhū son of Yehokal" (Driver, 1945 *lmqnyhw bn yhwmlk*; EEA, No.44) and on two bullae: *lṣfn[yhw] (son of) mqnyhw* "Belonging to Ṣefan[yāhū] (son of) Miqneyāhū" (Avigad, 1986, No.154) *lʾḥmlk (son of) mqnyhw* "Belonging to ʾAḥimelek (son of) Miqneyāhū (Deutsch, 1997, No.26).

The northern Israelite parallel of the name appears on the seal *lmyqnyw ʿbd yhwh* "Belonging to Miqneyaw/ō, servant of Yahweh" (Cross, 1983:55–63).

Sh. Moussaieff collection

Fig. 104. Judean bone seal belonging to "Miqneyāhū"

105.(28). **The seal of ʾAbiṭobiyāh**

The upper part of a bone seal, scaraboid and perforated, 17.3x8.9x9.0 mm. in size. Its surface is divided by a single line and surrounded by a ladder pattern.

The 7th century B.C.E. Hebrew inscription reads:

> **לאבטביה / ...**
> *lʾbṭbyh* / ...
> "Belonging to ʾAbiṭobiyāh (son of ...)"

ʾbṭbyh — ʾAbiṭobiyāh — A hitherto unrecorded composite theophoric personal name literally meaning "My good father is (the god) Yāhū". The OT records the names ʾAbiṭub (I Chr. 8:11) and Ṭobiyah (Ezra 2:66; Neh. 2:10,19, 3:35, 4:1 etc.). *ʾbyṭb* appears also in Aramaic of the Persian period (CIS II, 123:2). In Akkadian we find the names *Abi-ṭabu* and *abu-ṭab* (Stamm, 1980:69).

ʾb — "father", as an epithet of God appears on numerous Hebrew, Ammonite, Moabite and Phoenician seals and other inscription, but never, as the combination on our seal.

Ṭbyhw — is, as we see a frequent name in the OT and the epigraphic sources (Davies, 1991:359). Names as *ṭbʾ* (AHL, No.44), *ṭbʾl* (Ezra 4:7; Bordreuil and Lemaire, 1976, No.18) and *ṭbšlm* (Heltzer and Ohana, 1978:47; Deutsch, 1997, No.11) are also known. Yet, the name *ʾbṭbyh* "ʾAbiṭobiyāh" remain till now unique. The lower part of the seal is missing therefore the patronym has been lost.

G. Chaya collection

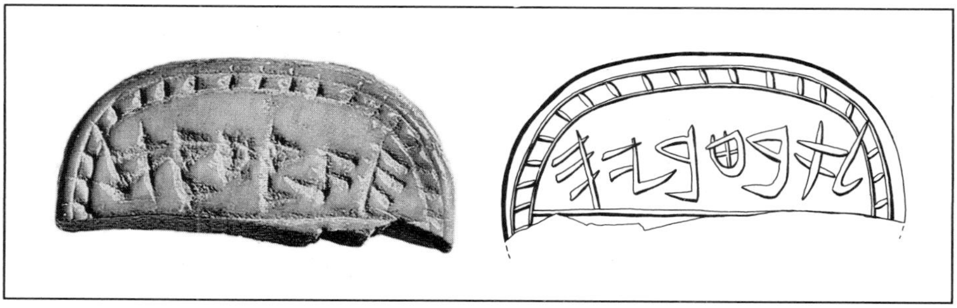

Fig. 105. Judean bone seal belonging to "ʾAbiṭobiyāh ...)"

Two Ammonite Seals

106.(29). The seal of ʾĒlīram the scribe

Dome shaped scaraboid white agate stone seal, lengthwise perforated and 24.8x14.5x12.6 mm. in size. The field is divided into four registers by three double lines. In the upper register an *anch* is depicted flanked by a star and the moon. In the lower register a stylized winged sun appears.

The Ammonite inscription reads:

לאליר/ם הספ/ר
lʾlyr/m hsp/r
"Belonging to ʾĒlīram the scribe"

ʾlyrm — ʾĒlīram, private name meaning "My God is high (exalted)" or "The God El elevates (me)". The letter *y* (yod) points toward the second proposal. The name *ʾlrm* without the letter *y* (yod) appears on three Ammonite seals: *lʾlrm bn tmʾ* (Aufrecht, 1989, No.15), *lʾlrm* (Ibid, No.28) and *lʿbdʾ nʿr ʾlrm* "Belonging to *ʿbdʾ*, attendant of *ʾlrm*" (Ibid, No.53). The names *ʾlrm*, and *ʾlyrm* appear also on a Hebrew seal: *lʾlrm (bn) ḥsdyhw* "Belonging to ʾEliram, son of Ḥasadyāhū" (Martin, 1964, No.3)

Sh. Moussaieff collection

Fig. 106. Ammonite agate seal belonging to "ʾĒlīram the scribe"

and two Hebrew bulla: *lʾlrm n... bn yrmy[hw]*"Belonging to ʾEliram, n... son of Yirmiyāhū" (Deutsch, 1997, No.32) and *lʾlyrm bn šmʿyhw* "Belonging to ʾEliram, son of Šemaʿayāhū" (Avigad, 1986, No.29). The name dos not occur in the OT but in its parallels such as *rmyh*, *ywrm* and *yhwrm* (II Chr. 17:8; II Reg. 1:17, 8:28 ; Ezra 10:25 etc.).

hsfr — "the scribe", a well known Biblical title (II Sam. 8:17; II Reg. 22:3,8–10 etc.). This is the second Ammonite seal of a scribe to be published. The previous one is: *lḥty sfr ʾdnr or ʾdn<n>r* "Belonging to *Ḥty* scribe of ʾAdnur or ʾAdoninur (the King?)" (Aufrecht, 1989, No.139). On royal scribes and their role see Avishur and Heltzer, 1996:40–46.

107.(30). **The seal of Šāʾūl**

Dome shaped scaraboid carnelian stone seal, lengthwise perforated and 12.8x11.1x8.0 mm. in size. The field is divided into two registers by a double line. In the upper register a crescent flanked by two dots is depicted.

The Ammonite inscription reads:

לשאל
lšʾl
"Belonging to Šāʾūl"

šʾl — The Biblical name Šāʾūl appears for the first time on the Ammonite seals. Two kings were named Šāʾūl, the first Israeli king of the united kingdom (I Sam. 9:2 etc.) and the sixth king of archaic Edom (Gen. 36:37; I Chr. 1:48 etc.). Šāʾūl was the name of other three men in the

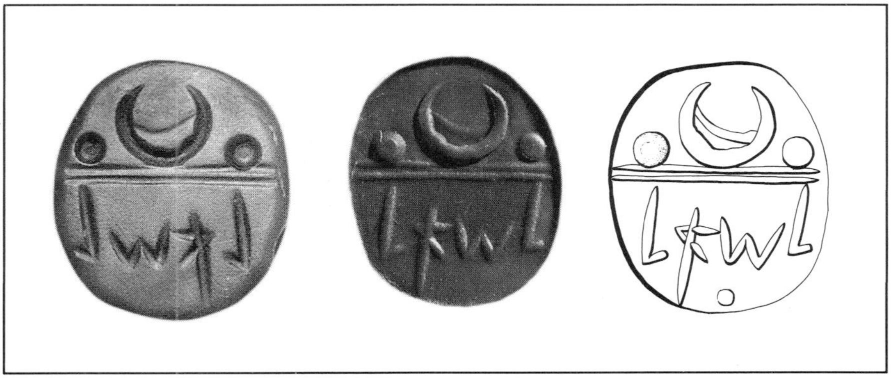

Fig. 107. Ammonite carnelian seal belonging to "Šāʾūl"

OT (Gen. 46:10; I Chr. 6:9; Ezra 10:29). The name Šā'ūl occurs on two Hebrew seals: *lšpṭ bn š'l* "Belonging to Šafaṭ, son of Šā'ūl" (AHL, No.87) and *l'ḥyw bn š'l* "Belonging to 'Aḥiyō, son of Šā'ūl" (Avigad, 1975, No.16). The name Šā'ūl' appears also in judeo-aramaic texts from Egypt (Maraqten, 1988:101, 214–5). The 4th century B.C.E. Wadi-Daliyeh papyri includes the name *yhwḥnn br š'lh* "Yehoḥanan, son of *Š'lh*" (Zsengeller, 1996:183). Here it is a passive participle with the meaning "The pleaded". A name suitable for a boy who comes after a long period of barrenness or after which only daughters were born in the family. A cognate name is *Š^e^alti'el* "I pleaded, asked from God" (Hag. 1:12,14, 2:2; I Chr. 3:17). There is also the 8th century B.C.E Phoenician inscription from Spain (Hispania 14) where two brothers *B'lytn* and *'bdb'l*, sons of *D'mlk* are defined as *bny Š'l* "pleaded sons" (IFPCO, 149–151, No.16).

Two Moabite Seals

108.(31). **The seal Mišpaṭ'ēl son of Ba'al'kš**

High dome shaped scaraboid agate stone seal, lengthwise perforated and 13.9x9.0x8.9 mm. in size. The field is divided into two registers by a single line and surrounded by a framing line. The left edge is damaged and therefore the letter *l* (lamed) is missing and the letter *b* (beth) is damaged, yet the reading is certain.

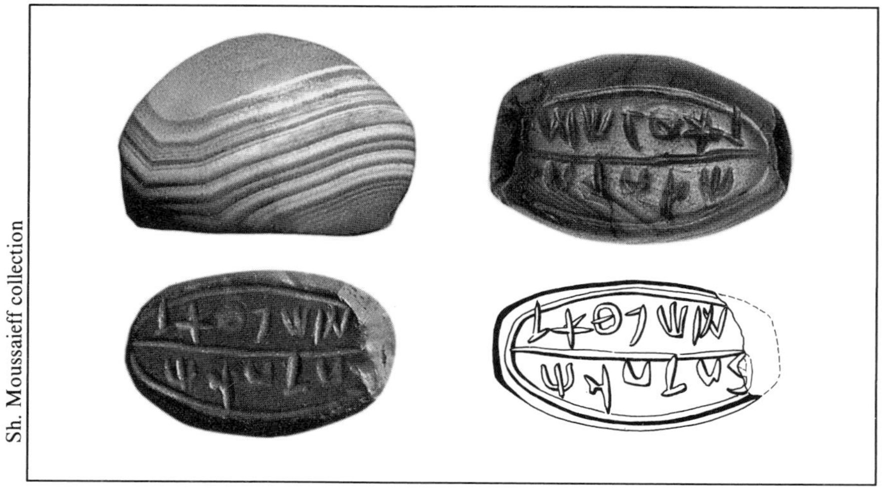

Fig. 108. Moabite agate seal belonging to "Mišpaṭ'ēl son of Ba'al'kš"

The inscription reads:

ל]משפטאל / בעלעכש]

lmšpṭ'l / bʿlʿkš

"[Belonging to] Mišpaṭ'ēl son of Baʿalʿkš"

The letters ʿ (ʿ*ayyin*) with the opening at the top, *m* (*mem*) and *š* (*shin*) are typical and similar to these which appear on three Moabite seals of the 6th century B.C.E.: 1) *lmšʿ* "Belonging to Mešaʿ", 2) *lmšʿ (bn) ʿd'l* "Belonging to Mešaʿ (son of) ʿ*d'l*", 3) *lmšpṭ* "Belonging to Mišpaṭ" (Hestrin and Dayagi, 1979, Nos. 115–117; Avigad, 1970a:291, No.8).

mšpṭ'l — The name is hitherto unrecorded. The hypocoristic name *mšpṭ* appears on the above mentioned seal and its meaning is "The justice of God". Hebrew parallels are *'lyšpṭ* (II Chr. 23:1) and *yhwšpṭ* (II Sam. 8:16; I Reg. 4:17, 15:24)

bʿlʿkš — Hitherto unrecorded theophoric name with the name of the god Baʿal. Therefore, the term ʿ*kš* has to describe the status or the action of the god. There is not known a root as ʿ*kš* in the west-semitic languages. In the OT we have the root ʿ*ks*, ʿekes (Jes. 3:18; Prov. 7:22), (also missing from the other west-semitic and Akkadian sources). It has the meaning "womans anklet". The text of Jes. 3:18 speaks about the taking away of various jewels, including the "womans anklet" — ʿ*ekes*. Moreover, we find in the OT the female name *ʿAksāh* (Jes. 15:16,17; Jud. 1:12,13; I Chr. 2:49). Therefore, a possible interpretation of the meaning of the name can be "The God Baʿal ornated".

109.(32). **The seal of Kemoš'ūr**

Reddish-brown hard stone seal, dome shaped scaraboid, unperforated and 27.5x25.7 mm. in size. Set in a bronze bezel. The lower edge is missing but both the iconography and the inscription are intact. The surface of the seal is dominated by a hybrid four winged deity which is flanked by three letters on each side forming the seals owner's name, all framed by a single framing line. The letters are large and deeply incised in high calligraphic style of the 8th century B.C.E.

The Moabite inscription reads:

לכמ/שאר

lkm/š'r

"Belonging to Kemoš'ūr"

The iconography, the four winged egyptian youth wearing a degenerated crown of the upper and lower Egypt is similar to these depicted on two other Moabite seals: 1) *lkmšṣdq* "Belonging to Kemošṣedeq" (Jakob-Rost, 1997:62–3, No.176), 2) *bʿlntn* "(Belonging to) Baʿalnātan" (Bordreuil, 1986:58, No. 61) as also, on several Phoenician seals (Gubel, 1993:125).

Fig. 109. Moabite stone seal belonging to "Kemošūʾr"

kmš'r — Typical Moabite name with the theophoric element *kmš* "Kemoš", the main Moabite god. This theophoric element appears in several Moabite names on seals such as: *kmš* "Kemoš" (Hestrin and Dayagi, 1972, No.114), *kmšdn* "Kemošdan" (Lemaire, 1983, No.11), *kmšyḥy* "Kemošyeḥi" (Bordreuil, 1986, No.66), *kmšm'š* (Avigad, 1970a:290–91), *kmšntn* (Avigad, 1970a:290), *lkmšṣdq* "Belonging to *Kmšṣdq*" (Jakob-Rost, 1997:62–3, No.176), *kmšḥsd hsfr* "Kemošḥasid the scribe" (NAAG, No.23) and on the bulla: *kmšʿz hsfr* "Kemošʿaz the scribe" (Avigad, 1992).

The element *'r* "light" appears for the first time in Moabite names (Timm, 1989), yet it is very common in Ammonite names (Aufrecht, 1989, Nos. 129,134,137,147). The name means "The God Kemoš is light (or lightens)".

A Phoenician Seal

110.(33). **The seal of ʿAbdimilk**

Dark red carnelian scarab seal, perforated and 13.3x9.5x6.2 mm. in size, set in a gold bezel. The seal surface is dominated by a griffin under which the inscription has been engraved from left to right in mirror-shape and in a positive manner.

The 8th century B.C.E. Phoenician inscription reads:

כלמדבע — (עבדמלך)

klmdbʿ — *(ʿbdmlk)* "(Belonging to) ʿAbdimilk"

Sh. Moussaieff collection

Fig. 110. Phoenician carnelian scarab seal in gold bezel belonging to "ʿAbdimilk"

ʿbdmlk — This is a very common Phoenician and Punic name (Benz, 1972:155, 344–5). *ʿbd-mlk* was the name (or the nickname, Deutsch, 1997:60) of the Biblical Kushi (man of Kush — Nubia) the eunuch (Jer. 38:7).

An Aramaic Seal

111.(34). **The seal of Barʾeyima**

Pink agate seal, dome shaped scaraboid, lengthwise perforated, 15.2x10.4x8.5 mm. in size. The seal surface is dominated by a sphinx standing to right with its forepart on-face spread wings and wearing a kilt. The aramaic inscription has been engraved into the empty space around the sphinx.

The 8th century B.C.E. inscription reads:

> **בראי/מ/ה**
> *brʾy/m/h*
> "(Belonging to) Barʾeyima" (vocalization questionable)

br — "son (of)" or "of (a quality)"

ʾymh — literary "fear, horror"

brʾymh — Barʾeyima, a new hitherto unrecorded name, not listed by Zadok (1988:408). A possible meaning of the name is "of fear", but from the other side it is possible, that the name by itself is not aramaic nor semitic, but of Asia Minor origin where the aramaic script or language has been used.

Fig. 111. Aramaic carnelian seal belonging to "Barʾeyima"

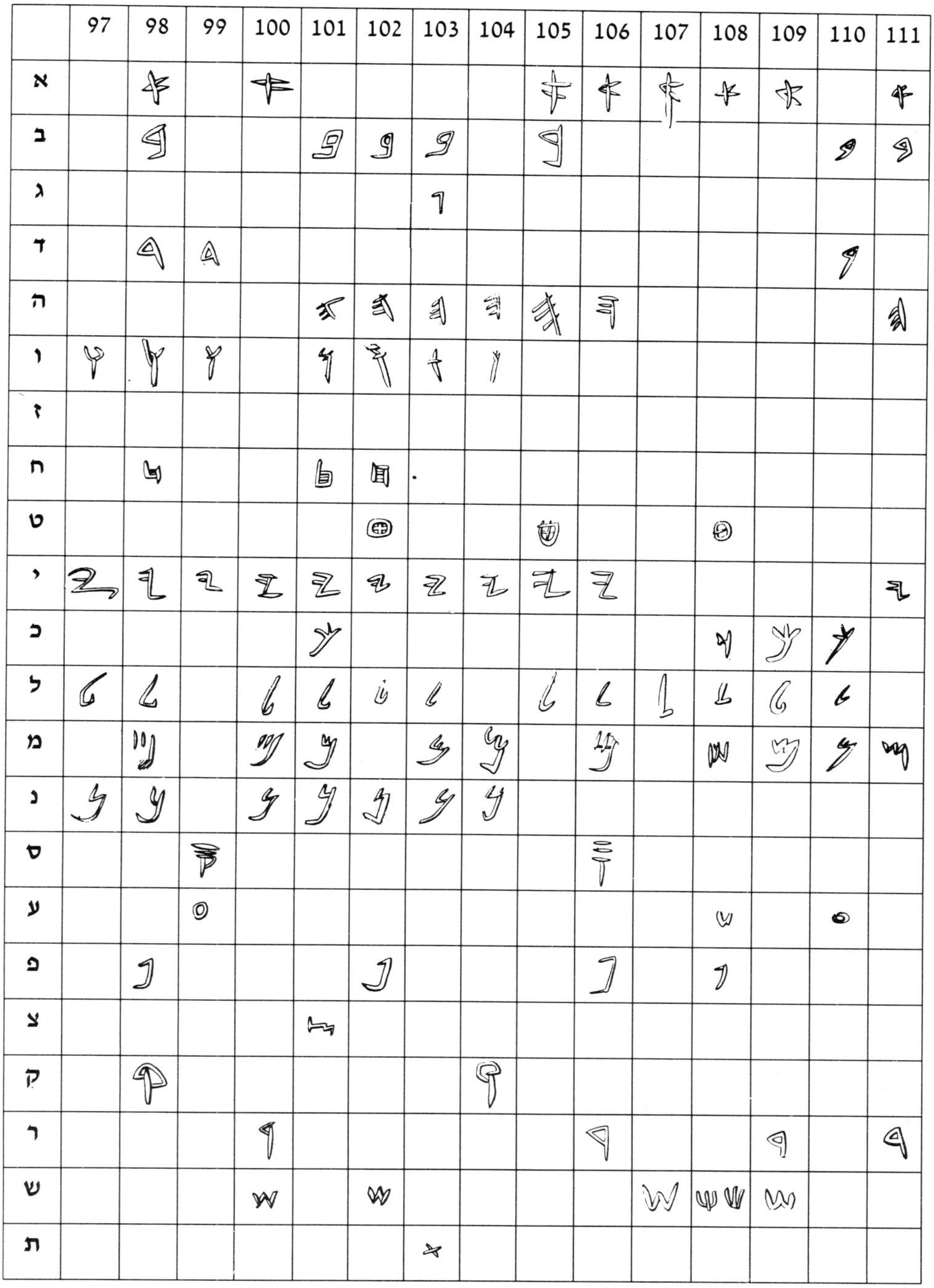

Pl. 3 Fifteen private seal inscriptions

AN INSCRIBED JUDEAN STORAGE JAR

112.(5). **A ceramic storage jar** of the Lachish III, 484 type, (*Lachish III*, Pl. 95, No. 484) which is well dated to the end of the eight century B.C.E. (Ussishkin, 1977:54–57). The jar is 58 cm. in height and its capacity is 48.6 liter. This is the standard type which usually bears the *lmlk* stamp on its handles. This jar does not bear the *lmlk* stamps, but instead, it has an inscription on the shoulder incised after firing. The height of the letters varies from 3.2 mm. to 1.0 mm. and the length of the inscription is 23.5 cm.

The inscription reads:

למלך שמן שפר =
lmlk šmn špr =

As also the jar, the inscription is to be dated paleographically to the end of the 8th century B.C.E.

lmlk — "belonging to the King" or "for the King"

šmn — "oil", probably olive oil designated or belonged to the King.

špr — This word appears for the first time in the epigraphic sources of the Iron Age III. According to the text it has to designate a certain quality of oil. In the OT the root *špr* has the meaning "to be beautiful, pleasing, good" (Gen.49:21; Daniel 3:32, 6:2, 4:24). In Palestinian Aramaic we find the word *š^{e}far* "the best". We can also use the verb "to beautify" i.e. to improve the quality (Sokoloff, 1992:564). The same meaning appears in the Talmudic literature and in Syriac (Levy, 1889:IV-599). Therefore we have to translate the word *špr* as "improved", "of high quality" or "best". Cf. also the expression *šemen ṭob* "good oil" (II Reg.20:13). The Aramaic-Greek bilingual inscription from Armazi (Georgia, in the Kaukasus) of the second century A.D. provide us with the expression: 9) *hkyn ṭb wšpyr yhwh hyk zy br ʾynš lʾ dnʿ* 10) *yhwh mn ṭbwt* "she was so nice and pleasant, that no person was her equal in beauty". We see here also the similarity of the meaning of the words *ṭwb* and *špyr* (DNWSI 1184–5).

= — 20 units, for a horizontal stroke means usually 10 in Hebrew and Phoenician (Renz and Rölling, 1995, II/I:49; Naveh, 1992:52–52).

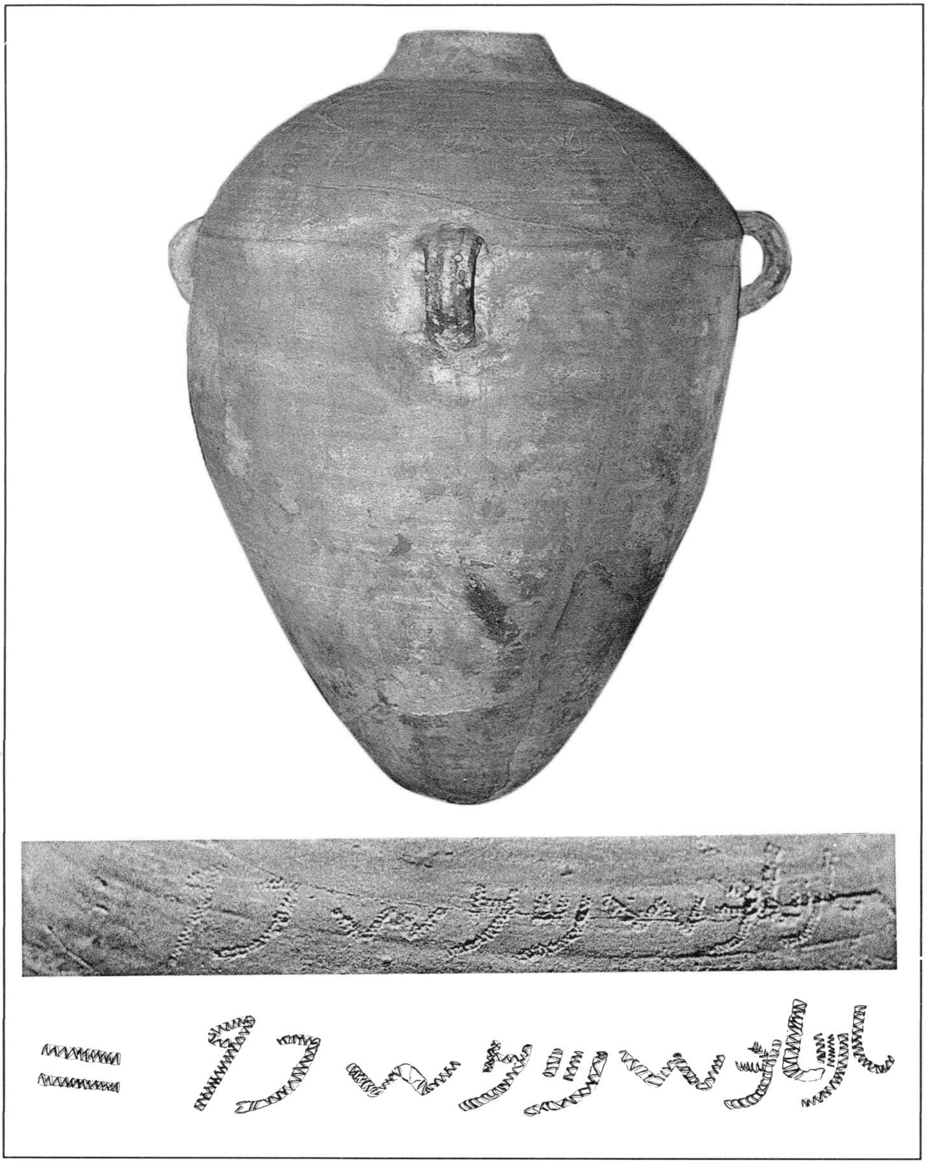

O. Golan collection

Fig. 112. Judean storage jar "belonging to the King"

Therefore we have here the designation of 20 units. The capacity of the jar, 48.6 liters, divided into 20 give us the value of 2.43 liter per one unit. We know that the Judean bat had the capacity of 21–24 liter (mostly 22.5 l., Renz and Röllig, 1995, II/I:36–38; Heltzer, 1989:195–208). A tenth of the *bat* was the *ʿiśśarōn* (Ibid.). Therefore we have here 20 *ʿiśśarōn's* = 2 *bat's*. This bring us to the following translation: "Belonging/for the King, good oil (of high quality), (quantity of) 20 ʿiśśarōn's".

AN INSCRIBED JUDEAN MEASUREMENT JUGLET

113.(6). **A ceramic measurement dipper juglet**, with a globular body and cylindrical neck pierced with two holes. The juglet is 7.5 cm. in height and its capacity to the bottom of its neck is 110 cm^3. On the shoulder, a Hebrew inscription has been incised before firing. The height of the letters varies from 1.8 mm. to 8.3 mm. and the length of the inscription is 7.8 cm.

The inscription reads:

> **להצליהו 0 בדד 1**
> *lhṣlyhw 0 bdd 1*

The letters are typical Judean and the inscription is to be dated paleographically to the end of the 7th century B.C.E.

hṣlyhw — Theophoric name meaning "The god Yāhū rescue, saved". The name is not found in the OT but is common in the Hebrew epigraphic material (Davies, 1991:336, recorded 11 times), and in a Judean ostraca *hṣlyhw bn bnyhw* (Deutsch and Heltzer, 1995, 79:18).

bdd 1 — lit. one single, one individual. In Arabic: a portion, a share, a part (Lane, 1863:161). The Biblical *qab* (II Reg.6,25), had the capacity of ca. 1.2 liters (Stern, 1962, 855). Therefore, *bdd* is probably the tenth part of a *qab*, or 1/20 of the *ʿiśśarōn* (?).

Therefore we offer the following translation: "Belonging to Hiṣṣilyāhū One portion, share".

Ch. Kaufman collection

Fig. 113. Judean measurement juglet belonging to "Hiṣṣilyāhū"

AN INSCRIBED JUDEAN JAR HANDLE

114. **Naḥūm (son of) ʾAḥʾimh, for (to, of) Semakyāhū**

Light brown ceramic jar handle (not 484 *lmlk* type), inscribed with 15 letters incised before firing (Fig. 114). The height of the letters varies from 3.8 mm. (the letter *y* yod) up to 11.2 mm. (the letter *s* samech). The inscription is 10.3 cm. long. The first three letters are written from the top toward the bottom after which the scribe had changed its axis with 90° and continues from the right to the left. The lower part of the handle is missing but the inscription is entire except for the last letter *w* (waw) which is damaged.

The Hebrew inscription reads:

נחם אחאמה לסמכיהו̇
nḥm ʾḥʾmh lsmkyhẇ
"Naḥūm (son of) ʾAḥʾimōh, to (for, of) Semakhyāhū"

There are three chronologicaly indicative letters which date the handle to the 7th century B.C.E., the two letters *m* (mem) with the dropped right shoulder, the letter s (samech) with the diagonal connecting line and the letter *h* (he) with the prominent top horizontal line.

nḥm — "Naḥūm" The biblical name (I Chr. 4:19) is a hypocoristicon of the name *Neḥemyā* (Ezra 2:2; Neh. 3:16). Neḥemyā is the name of the governor of Judah in the time of Artaxerxes I, from 445 B.C.E. and Naḥūm is the name of the biblical prophet. The name is very common in the Hebrew epigraphy and has been recorded 23 times by Davies (1991:439) and once by Deutsch (1997, No. 64).

The phenomenon of inscribed handles before firing is known from Gibeon (Pritchard, 1959).

ʾḥʾmh — "ʾAḥʾimoh" literary "his mother "s brother". In the OT we find the shortened name "ʾAḥīʾām" (II Sam. 23:33; I Chr. 11:35). The name appears twice in the Hebrew epigraphy, on the seal of *ʾḥʾmh bn yqmyhw* "ʾAḥʾimōh son of Yeqamyāhū" (Bordreuil and Lemaire, 1976,

No.8) and on the bulla of *pšḥr bn ʾḥʾmh* — "Pašḥur son of ʾAḥʾimōh" (Avigad, 1986, No. 151).

smkyhw — "Semakhyāhū" Theophoric name meaning "Yāhū will protect". The name is known from the OT (I Chr. 26:7) and from the Hebrew epigraphic material, recorded 8 times in its full spelling and 14 times in its shortened forms: *smk*, *smky* and *smkyh* (Davies, 1991:448–9; Deutsch, 1997, No. 68,69,96). Parallels, where the inscriptions are written on the handles before firing are found at Gibeon from the VII century B.C.E. (Pritchard, 1955, Nos. 21–25) and a jar handle fragment bearing the inscription *[ʾl]nqm / gdl[yhw]* (Prignaud, 1070:50–59).

The inscription is unusual and unique. It can have the following interpretation: "The vessel belonged to Naḥum, the son of Aḥʾimo, who is of the Samakyāhū family (or clan)", i.e. the prefix *l* (lamed) can have also the sense "belonging to the family (clan)".

Sh. Moussaieff collection

Fig. 114. Judean inscribed jar handle "Naḥum (son of) ʾAḥʾimōh, to (for, of) Semakhyāhū"

A HEBREW SEAL IMPRESSION ON A JAR HANDLE

115. Ḥaggay (son of) Ḥabay

Ceramic jar handle of the 484 *lmlk* type, bearing a seal impression, 16.3x13.1 mm. in size (Fig. 115). The inscription includes six letters divided into two lines of three letters.

The Hebrew inscription reads:

חבי / חגי
ḥby / ḥgy
"(Belonging to) Ḥaby (or Ḥabbay), (son of) Ḥaggay"

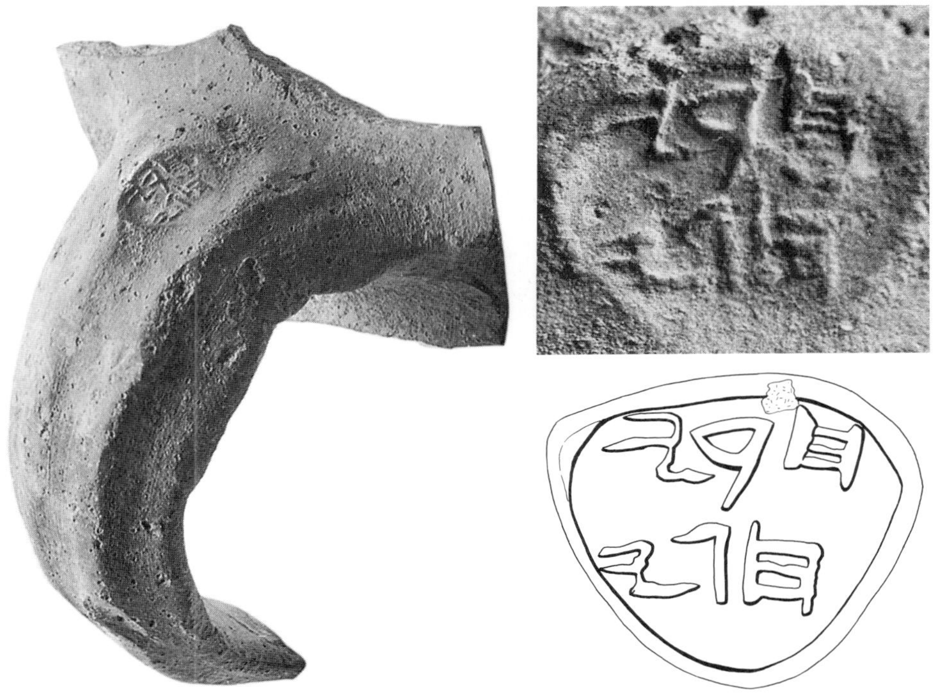

Sh. Moussaieff collection

Fig. 115. Judean private seal impression on a jar handle belonging to "Ḥabbay, (son of) Ḥaggay"

ḥby — "Ḥaby (or Ḥabbay)" Theophoric hypocoristicon known from the OT in its more complete form *ḥbyh* "Ḥabyāh" (Ezra 2:61; Neh. 7:63). Avigad (1988, No.52) published a bulla: *lḥbʾ b/n mtn* "Belonging to *Ḥbʾ*, son of Mattan". He argues that the root is *ḥbʾ* "to hide, to make confidently". The full theophoric name with the root *ḥbʾ* is *ʾElyaḥbāʾ* (II Sam.23:32; I Chr.11:33). See also the name *Yeḥubbā* (I Chr.7:34). The full name as Avigad points out (1988:49) had to be **Ḥabayāhū*. The name appears also on three bullae: *lʾḥyqm / bn ḥby* "Belonging to ʾAḥiqam, son of Ḥaby" (Supra Nos. 94.a-c) and seven identical fragmentary bullae are on display at the Hecht Museum (AHL, in press).

ḥgy — "Ḥaggay" literary "My feast-day". Private name widely known from the OT (Gen. 46:16; Num. 26:15) and it is also the name of the prophet Ḥaggay. The name is common in the Hebrew Epigraphy and has been recorded 9 times by Davies (1991:347), once by Deutsch and Heltzer (1995:83, 77:2), once by Overbeck and Meshorer (1993:8, No. 33) and once by Deutsch (1997, No. 51).

	112	113	114	115
א			⟨glyph⟩	
ב		⟨glyph⟩		⟨glyph⟩
ג				⟨glyph⟩
ד		⟨glyph⟩		
ה		⟨glyph⟩	⟨glyph⟩	
ו		⟨glyph⟩		
ז				
ח			⟨glyph⟩ ⟨glyph⟩	⟨glyph⟩
ט				
י		⟨glyph⟩		⟨glyph⟩
כ	⟨glyph⟩			
ל	⟨glyph⟩	⟨glyph⟩		
מ	⟨glyph⟩		⟨glyph⟩ ⟨glyph⟩	
נ	⟨glyph⟩		⟨glyph⟩	
ס				
ע				
פ	⟨glyph⟩			
צ		⟨glyph⟩		
ק				
ר	⟨glyph⟩			
ש	⟨glyph⟩			
ת				

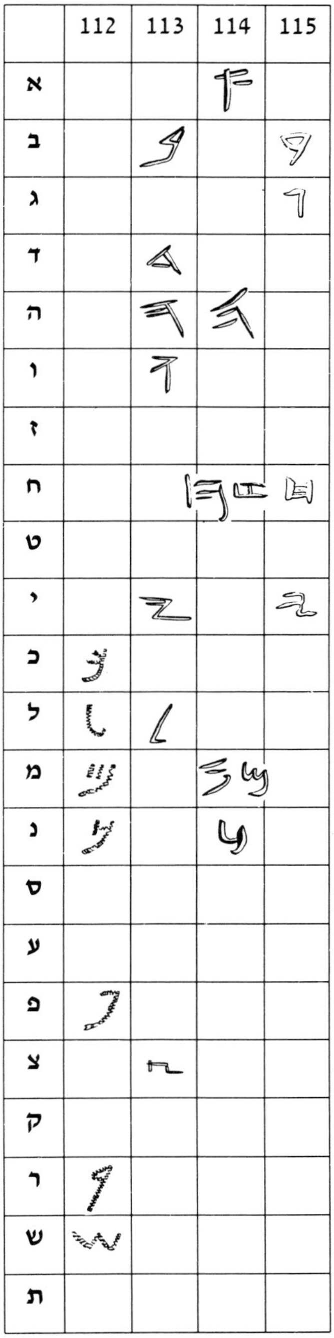

Pl. 4 Storage jar, measurement juglet and handle inscriptions

AN ARAMAIC SEAL IMPRESSION ON A BODY SHERD

116. Yehud, Malkiyāū

A seal impression on a body sherd of a jar (Fig.116).[1] The seal impression size is 21.3x18.7 mm. The lower right corner is missing. The Aramaic script is divided into two registers by a single line.

The inscription read:

> **יהוד / [מ]לכיו**
> *yhwd / [m]lkyw*
> "Yehud, Malkiyāū"

yhwd — This is the name of the province of Yehud. The "Yehud" seal impressions from Judah of the Persian period are well known (Avigad, 1976; Naveh, 1982:116; Stern, 1982:203).

[m]lkyw, "Malkiyau or Malkiyō" — The name with the suffix *yw* instead of *yhw* is characteristic to the Northern, i.e. Israelite personal names, yet, it occasionally appears also in Judah in the preexilic times, as also in the Persian period. In the OT the name appears only with the southern theophoric suffix *yh*, *yhw* (Neh.3:14, 3:31, 8:4, 10:4, 12:42; Jer.38:6 etc.). *Mlkyw* is unknown from the pre-Exilic epigraphic material and this is the second seal impression bearing this inscription. Yet, the first seal impression found at Tell Nimrîn in Jordan (16 Km. eastward of Jericho, Dempsey, 1996:77), is not identical with the one presented above and has been sealed with a different seal, probably belonging to the same person. These are official seals of the province of Judah which where used to seal ceramic vessels. The impressions are usually found on the body and the handles of the jars impressed before firing. The list of seal impressions found in Judah, which mentions the name of the province *Yhwd* and the name or the title of the governor follows:

---

1 The item has been purchased by the collector in Jerusalem from an antiquities dealer.

1. *yhwd* / *ʾwryw* — (Jericho, Avigad, 1957)
2. *yhwd* / *ḥnnh* — (Ramat Rahel, p. 46, Pl. 20, 7)
3. *yhwd* / *yhwʿzr* / *pḥwʾ* — (Ramat Rahel, p. 44, 1, Pl. 20, 9)
4. *yhwd* (or *yhd*) / *hpḥh* — (Ramat Rahel, p. 45, Pl. 20, 1–2)
5. *yhwd* / *mlkyw* — (From Tell Nimrîn in Jordan, Dempsey, 1996:77)
6. *yhwd* / *[m]lkyw* — (The above with unrecorded provenance)
7. *lḥnwnh* / *yhwd* — (Two probably identical stamps, one from Tel Harasim and the second from Babylon, belonging probably to a woman, Naveh, 1996:45)
8. *yʾz* / *br yšb* / *yhwd* (sic) (From Belmont Castle, Millard, 1989; Naveh, 1996:45)

And as an analogy to the *yhwd* seals we have to add the province of *ʿmn* stamp:

9. *šbʾ* / *ʿmn* (From Tell el-ʿUmeiri, Herr, 1992; Heltzer, 1995: 70–72)

On seal no. 4 *yhwd (*or *yhd)* / *hpḥh* the name is missing and it seems that the seal belonged to the administration of the provincial governor. The names *ʾwryw*, *ḥnnh* and *mlkyw* appear without the title and the fact, that *ḥnnh* was a woman as it is pointed out by Naveh (1996:45–6), seems to show, that *ʾwryw*, *ḥnnh* and *mlkyw* were possibly not governors but high officials in the provincial administration.

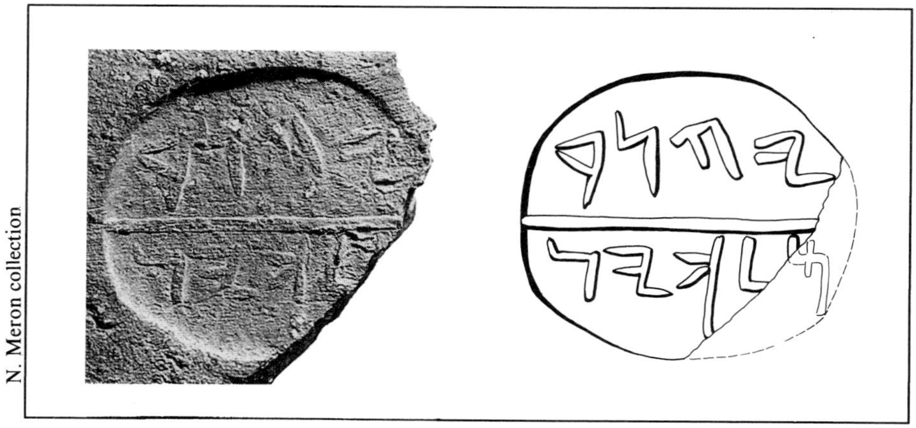

Fig. 116. Judean Aramaic seal impression on a body sherd — "Yehud, Malkiyāū"

FOUR JUDEAN WEIGHTS

117. (6). **Neṣef stone weight**

Dome-shaped, inscribed reddish steatite stone weight, 9.4 gr. (Fig. 117). Height: 17.6 mm., max. diameter:20.4 mm.

The Hebrew inscription reads:

נצף — *nṣf*
"Neṣef".

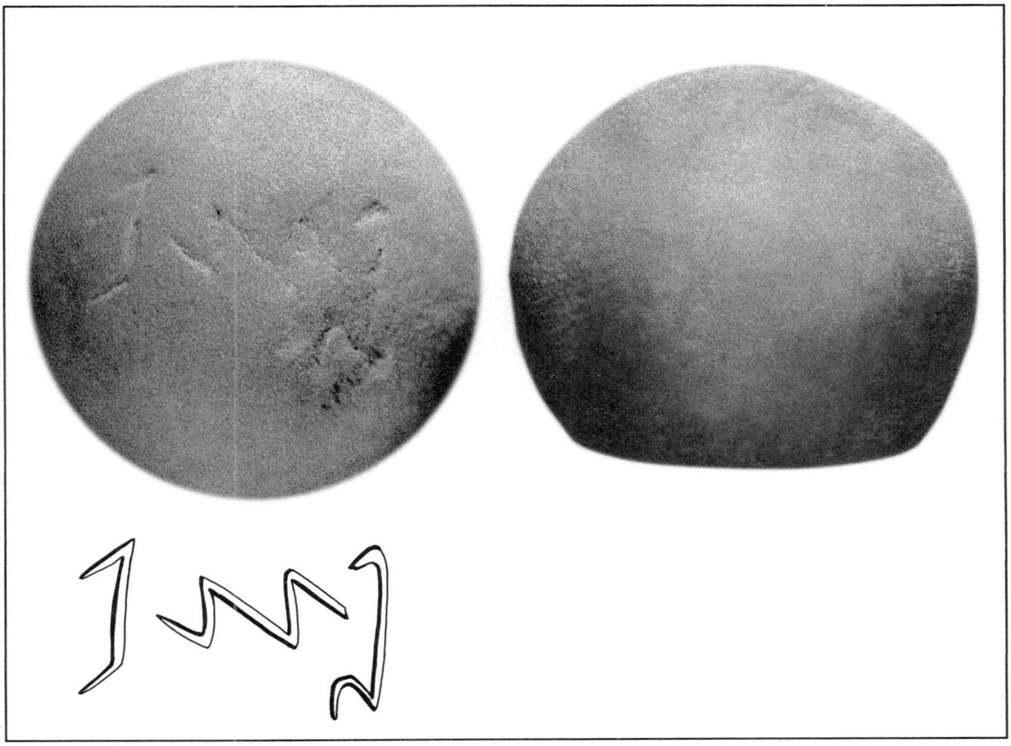

G. Chaya collection

Fig. 117. Stone weight "Neṣef"

Fig. 118. Stone weight "One shekel"

The first letter *n* (nun) has been incised inverted. 52 weights of the *neṣef* type are recorded, 51 by Kletter (1991:146-8) and one by Deutsch and Heltzer (1994:65), with the value of 20/24 of a shekel. In general the weight of the *neṣef* is varying from 8.24 gr. (only in one case 7.97 gr.) to 10.5 gr. (only in one case 11.23 gr.) (Kletter, 1991:144–7). The above presented *neṣef* weight is exactly 83% (20/24) from the average Judean shekel which weights 11.33 gr (Ibid, p. 134). It is noteworthy that the *neṣef* is also similar in weight with the Egyptian *kit (kidet)* of 9.1 gr. (Helck, 1980) and to the second millennium B.C.E. Ugaritic shekel of 9–9.9gr. (Parise, 1971; 1981:154–160 with the average of 9.4 gr) which belong to three different measurement systems.

118.(7). **Stone weight of one Shekel**

Dome-shaped, inscribed black-reddish steatite stone weight, 11.33 gr. (Fig. 118). Height: 17.7 mm., max. diameter: 20.5 mm.

İ Ẏ

"One Y (The sign Y stands for *Shekel*)".

On the flat bottom, a winged sun with a crescent and two stars are engraved. This points toward an Ammonite origin. The iconography, is possibly a Royal one. The value of 11.33 gr., has been proposed as the average value for the Judean dome-shaped weight (Kletter, 1991:134). 35 Judean weights with the value of one shekel are recorded by Kletter (Ibid:140–1) and no one has the exact weight of 11.33 gr. Therefore, the weight presented here could be a Royal prototype of the sheqel. The iconography also points out that the weight of the Judean sheqel has been adopted also in the Ammonite Kingdom.

119.(8). **Bronze weight of one Shekel**

Cubic, inscribed bronze weight, 11.27 gr. (Fig. 119). Height: 9.0 mm., top:13.5x12.0 mm.

On the flat surface, the value is marked:

1Y

"One shekel".

Bronze inscribed weights of the Shekel type are rare and are always cubic or trapezoidal in shape opposite to the Judean stone dome-shaped weights (with one exception, Deutsch and Heltzer, 1994:65–6). Kletter (1991:121) recorded six metal examples to which are to be added five published by Deutsch and Heltzer (1994:63–8) and two presented here, a total of 13 metal weights. Our shekel weights 11.27 gr. which is very close to the average of 11.33 gr. suggested by Kletter (1991:134).

120.(9). **Bronze weight of four Shekels**

Trapezoidal, inscribed bronze weight, 45.10 gr. (Fig. 120). Height: 14.1 mm., top: 21.0x19.8 mm.

The top is marked with the value:

4Ꮍ
"Four shekels".

Another bronze inscribed weight of the shekel type with the average of 11.27 gr. for the shekel (see the previous weight with the same shekel value), similar in shape to these of the *lmlk II*, and *lmlk ᎩII* weights, the first found at Gezer and the second without known provenance (Gezer II:285, fig.433; Deutsch and Heltzer, 1994:66–7, Fig.32).

Fig. 119. Bronze weight "One shekel"

Fig. 120. Bronze weight "Four shekels"

BIBLIOGRAPHY

ADAJ — Annual of the Department of Antiquities of the Hashemite Kingdom of Jordan.

AHL — Avigad, N., Heltzer, M. and Lemaire, A. *A Catalogue of the West Semitic Seals in the Hecht Collection.* Haifa. (in print).

AHW — von Soden, W. 1959–1981. *Akkadisches Handwörterbuch I–III.* Wiesbaden.

Aharoni, Y. (et al.) 1962. *Excavations at Ramat Raḥel, Seasons 1959 and 1960.* Roma.

Aharoni, Y. (et al.) 1964. *Excavations at Ramat Raḥel, Seasons 1961 and 1962.* Roma.

Aharoni, Y. 1968. Trial Excavations in the "Solar Shrine" at Lachish. Preliminary Report. *IEJ* 18:157–169.

Aharoni, Y. 1978. *Arad Inscriptions.* Jerusalem.

Aufrecht, W.E. 1989, *A Corpus of Ammonite Inscriptions.* Lewiston, Queenston, Lampeter.

AUSS — Andrews University Seminary Studies.

Avigad, N. 1954. Seven Ancient Hebrew Seals. *BIES* 18:145–153. (Hebrew).

Avigad, N. 1957. A New Class of *Yehud* Stamps. *IEJ* 7:146–153.

Avigad, N. 1970. Six Ancient Hebrew Seals, *Sefer Shmuel Yeivin.* Jerusalem. 305–308. (Hebrew).

Avigad, N. 1970. Ammonite and Moabite Seals, in Sanders, J.A. (ed.) 1970. *Near Eastern Archaeology in the Twentieth Century: Essays in Honor of Nelson Glueck.* Garden City, N.Y.

Avigad, N. 1975. New Names on Hebrew Seals. *EI* 12:66–71. (Hebrew).

Avigad, N. 1975a. The Priest of Dor. *IEJ* 25:101–105.

Avigad, N. 1976. Bullae and Seals from a Post-Exilic Judean Archive. *Qedem* 4. Jerusalem.

Avigad, N. 1978. The Kings Daughter and the Lyre. *IEJ* 28:146–151.

Avigad, N. 1979. A Group of Hebrew Seals from the Hecht Collection, in: *Festschrift Rëuben R. Hecht* (no editor). Jerusalem:119–126.

Avigad, N. 1981. Titles and Symbols on Hebrew Seals. *EI* 15:303–305. (Hebrew).

Avigad, N. 1986. *Hebrew Bullae from the Time of Jeremiah*. Jerusalem.

Avigad, N. 1987. The Contribution of Hebrew Seals to an Understanding of Israelite Religion and Society. in P. D. Miller, P. D. Hanson and D. S. McBride (eds.). *Ancient Israelite Religion. Essays in Honor of F.M. Cross*. Philadelphia:195–208.

Avigad, N. 1988. The Seals of Neriyahu, the Kings Son, in Mirsky, A., Grossman, A. and Kaplan, Y. (eds.) 1988. *Exile and Diaspora; Studies in the History of the Jewish People Presented to Prof. H. Beinart*. Jerusalem.

Avigad, N. 1992. A New Seal of a "Son of the King". *Michmanim* 6:27*–31*.

Avigad, N., Heltzer, M. and Lemaire, A. *A Catalogue of the West Semitic Seals in the Hecht Collection*. Haifa. (in print).

Avishur, Y and Heltzer, M. 1996. *Studies on the Royal Administration in Ancient Israel in the Light of Epigraphic Sources*. Jerusalem. (Hebrew).

BA — Biblical Archaeologist.

Barkay, G. 1993. A Bulla of Ishmael, the King's Son, *BASOR* 290–91:109–14.

BASOR — Bulletin of the American Schools of Oriental Research.

Beit-Arieh, I. and Cresson, B. 1985. An Edomite Ostracon From Ḥorvat ʿUza. *Tel Aviv* 12:96–101.

Benz, F.L. 1972. *Personal Names in the Phoenician and Punic Inscriptions*. Rome.

BIES — Bulletin of the Israel Exploration Society. (Hebrew). (Yediʿot).

BMB — Bulletin du Musée de Beyrouth.

Bordreuil, P. 1982. Épigraphes phéniciennes sur bronze, sur pierre et sur ceramique, *Archeologie en Levant*, Recueil R. Saidah. 188–192.

Bordreuil, P. 1985. Inscriptions sigillaires ouest-sémitiques III, Sceaux de dignitaires et de rois syro-palestiniens du VIIIe et du VIIe siècle avant J.-C., *Syria* 62:21–29.

Bordreuil, P. 1986. *Catalogue des Sceaux Ouest Sémitiques inscrits de la Bibliotheque Nationale du Musée de Louvre et du Musée biblique de Bible et Terre Sainte*. Paris.

Bordreuil, P. 1986a. A Note on the seal of Peqaḥ the Armor-Bearer, Future King of Israel, *BA* 49:54–55.

Bordreuil, P. 1992. Fléches phéniciennes inscrites: 1981–1991 I. *RB* 100:203–213.

Bordreuil, P. and Lemaire, A. 1976. Nouveaux sceaux hébreux, araméens et ammonites. *Semitica* 26:45–63.

Bordreuil, P. and Lemaire, A. 1979. Nouveaux group de sceaux hébreux, araméens et ammonites. *Semitica* 29:71–84.

CAI — Aufrecht, W.E. 1989. *A Corpus of Ammonite Inscriptions*. Lewiston, Queenston Lampeter.

CIS — Corpus Inscriptionum Semiticarum.

Cross, F.M. 1980. Newly Found Inscriptions in Old Canaanite and Early Phoenician Inscriptions. *BASOR* 238:1–20.

Cross, F.M. 1983. The Seal of *Miqneyaw*, servant of Yahweh. ed. Gorelick L. and Williams-Forte E. *Ancient Seals and the Bible*. Malibu:55–63.

Cross, F.M. 1992. A Newly Discovered Inscribed Arrowheads of the Eleventh Century B.C.E., *IMJ* 10:57–62.

Cross, F.M. 1993. A Newly Discovered Inscribed Arrowhead of the 11th Century B.C.E. In *Biblical Archaeology Today 1990. Proceeding of the Second International Congress of Biblical Archaeology*. Jerusalem:533–542.

Cross, F.M. 1995. A Note on a Recently Published Arrowhead. *IEJ* 45:188–189.

Cross, F.M. 1996. The Arrow of Suwar, Retainer of ʿAbday, *EI* 25:9*–17*.

Cross, F.M. and Milik, J.T. 1956. A Typological Study of the El Khader Javelin and Arrow-Heads, *ADAJ* III:15–23.

Crowfoot, J.W., Crowfoot, G.M. and Kenyon, K. 1957. *Samaria-Sebaste* 3. London.

Davies, G.I. 1991. *Ancient Hebrew Inscriptions: Corpus and Concordance*. Cambridge.

DdA — Dialoghi di Archeologia.

Del Olmo Lete, G. and Sanmartin, J. 1996. *Diccionario de la Lengua Ugaritica* I. Barcelona.

Dempsey, D. 1996. Ostraca and a Seal Impression from Tell Nimrîn, Jordan. *BASOR* 303:73–78.

Deutsch, R. 1997. *Messages from the Past, Hebrew Bullae from the Time of Isaiah Through the Destruction of the First Temple.* Tel Aviv-Jaffa. (Hebrew).

Deutsch, R. and Heltzer, M. 1994. *Forty New Ancient West Semitic Inscriptions.* Tel Aviv-Jaffa.

Deutsch, R. and Heltzer, M. 1995. *New Epigraphic Evidence from the Biblical Period.* Tel Aviv-Jaffa.

Deutsch, R. and Heltzer, M. 1997. ʿAbday on Eleventh-Century B.C.E. Arrowheads. *IEJ* 47:111–2.

DHL — Overbeck, B. and Meshorer, Y. 1993. *Das heilige Land: Antike Münzen und Siegel aus einem Jahrtausend jüdischer Geschichte.* Catalog der Sonderausstellung. München.

DNWSI — Hoftijzer, J. and Jongeling, K., 1995. *Dictionary of North-West Semitic Inscriptions.* Leiden.

Driver, G.R. 1945. A New Israelite Seal, *PEQ* 77:5.

EB — *Encyclopedia Biblica* I–VIII. Jerusalem. 1952–1982. (Hebrew).

EEA — Moscati S. 1951. *L'Epigraphia Ebraica Antica.* Roma.

EI — *Eretz-Israel,* Archaeological, Historical and Geographical Studies. Jerusalem.

EV — *Epigrafika Vostoka.* (Russian)

Fales, F.M. 1986. *Aramaic Epigraphs on Clay Tablets of the Neo-Assyrian Period.* Roma.

Fowler, J.D. 1988. *Theophoric Personal Names in Ancient Hebrew, A Comparative Study.* Sheffield.

Geraty, L.T. 1985. The Andrews University Madaba Plains Project, A Preliminary Report on the First Season at Tell el-ʿUmeiri, *AUSS* 23:85–110.

Gezer II — Mecalister, R.A.S. 1912. *The Excavations of Gezer II.* London.

Gubel, E. 1993. The Iconography of Inscribed Phoenician Glyptic. in: *SINSIS*: 101–129.

Guigues, P.E. 1926. Pointe de fléche en bronze a inscription phénicienne. *MUSJ* 11:325–328.

Hazor II — Yadin, Y. et al., 1959. *Hazor II.* Jerusalem.

Helck, W. 1980. *Lexikon der Egyptologie.* Masse und Gewichte, pp. 1199–1209.

Heltzer, M. 1978. *Goods, Prices and the Organization of Trade in Ugarit.* Wiesbaden.

Heltzer, M. 1982. *The Internal Organization of the Kingdom of Ugarit.* Wiesbaden.

Heltzer, M. 1989. Some Questions of the Ugaritic Metrology and its Parallels in Judah, Phoenicia, Mesopotamia and Greece. *UF* 21:195–208.

Heltzer, M. 1992. *Die Organisation des Handwerks, im "Dunkelem Zeitalter" und im I Jahrtausend v.u.Z. im östlichen Mittelmeergebiet.* Padova.

Heltzer, M. 1995. Zu einem Verwaltungsproblem in den Provinzen der V Satrapie des Achämenidenreiches. *AOF* 22:70–72.

Heltzer, M. and Ohana M. 1978. *The Extra-Biblical Tradition of Hebrew Personal Names.* Haifa. (Hebrew).

Herr, L.G. 1985. The Servant of Baalis, *BA* 48:169–172.

Herr, L.G. 1992. Two Stamped Impressions of the Persian Province of Ammon from Tell el-ʿUmeiri, *ADAJ* 26:163–166.

Herr, L.G. 1992a. Epigraphic Finds from Tell el-ʿUmeiri During the 1989 Seasons, *AUSS* 30:187–200.

Hestrin, R. and Dayagi-Mendels, M. 1979. *Inscribed Seals, First Temple Period.* Jerusalem.

Hess, R.S. 1993. *Amarna Personal Names.* Winona Lake.

Horn, S.H. 1968. An Inscribed Seal from Jordan, *BASOR* 189:41–43.

IEJ — Israel Exploration Journal.

IFPCO — Guzzo-Amadasi, M.G. 1967. *Le iscrizioni fenici e punichi delle colonie in occidente.* Roma.

IMJ — Israel Museum Journal.

Jakob-Rost, L. 1997. *Die Stempelsiegel im Vorderasiatischen Museum Berlin.* Mainz.

JNES — Journal of Near Eastern Studies.

KAI — Donner, H. and Röllig, W. 1964. *Kanaanäische und aramäische Inschriften* I–III. Wiesbaden.

Kletter, R. 1991. The Inscribed Weights of the Kingdom of Judah. *Tel-Aviv* 18:121–163.

Kraus, F. 1984. *Königliche Verfügungen in altbabylonischer Zeit.* Leiden.

Lachish III, — Tuffnel, O. (et al.) 1953. *Lachish III, The Iron Age.* London. (Epigraphic chapter written by D. Diringer)

Lane, E.W. 1863, *Arabic English Lexicon*, Beiruth. Vol. I (Reprint 1968).

Lemaire, A. 1979. Note sur le titre *BN HMLK* dans l'ancient Israël, *Semitica* 29:59–65.

Lemaire, A. 1982. Notes d'épigraphie nord-ouest sémitique. *Semitica* 32:19.

Lemaire, A. 1983. Nouveaux sceaux nord-ouest sémitiques. *Semitica* 33:17–31.

Lemaire, A. 1985. Sept sceaux nord-ouest sémitiques inscrits. *EI* 18:29*–32*.

Lemaire, A. 1986. Nouveaux sceaux nord-ouest sémitiques. *Syria* 63:305–325.

Lemaire, A. 1989. Nouvelle pointe de fléche inscrite proto-phénicienne. *SEL* 6:53–56.

Lemaire, A. 1995. Épigraphie Palestinienne: Nouveaux documents, II — Décennie 1985–1995. *Henoch* XVII:209–242.

Levy, J. 1889. *Neuhebräisches und chaldäisches Wörterbuch uber die Talmudim und Midraschim* I–IV. Leipzig.

Lipinsky, E. 1995. *Dieux et déesses de l'univers phénicien et punique. OLA* 64.

Liverani, M. 1971. Συδυκ e Μιςωρ, *Studi E. Volterra* VI:55–74.

Loewenstamm, Sh. 1958. Ḥeleṣ. *EB* III:159–160. (Hebrew).

Maraqten, M. 1988. *Die semitischen Personennamen in den alt- und reichsaramischen Inschriften aus Vorderasien*. Hildesheim.

Martin, M.F. 1962. A Twelfth Century Bronze Palimpsest. *RSO* 37:175–197.

Martin, M.F. 1964. Six Palestinian Seals. *RSO* 39:203–210.

McCarter, P.K. Jr. 1996. Pieces of the Puzzle, *Biblical Archaeology Review* 22/2:39–43, 62–63.

Milik, J.T. and Cross F.M. 1954. Inscribed Javelin Heads from the Period of the Judges, A Recent Discovery in Palestine. *BASOR* 134:5–15.

Milik, J.T. 1956. An Unpublished Arrow-Head with Phoenician Inscription of the 11th–10th Century B.C.E. *BASOR* 143:3–6.

Milik, J.T. 1961. Fléches a inscriptions phéniciennes au Musée National Libanais. *BMB* 16:103–108, Pl.I.

Millard, A. 1989. Notes on Two Seal Impressions on Pottery. *Levant* 21:60–61.

Mitchell, T.C. 1985. Another Palestinian Inscribed Arrowhead, in Palestine in the Bronze and Iron Ages. *Papers in Honor of Olga Tufnell*. London:136–153.

MUSJ — *Mélanges de l'Université Saint-Josephe*, Beyrouth.

NAAG — Numismatic and Ancient Art Gallery, Auction catalogue No. 7. Zürich.

Naveh, J. 1982. *Early History of the Alphabet*. Jerusalem.

Naveh, J. 1992. The Numbers of Bat in the Arad Ostraca, *IEJ* 42:52–54.

Naveh, J. 1996. Gleanings of Some Pottery Inscriptions, *IEJ* 46:44–51.

NFA — Classical Auctions, Inc., *Egyptian Near Eastern Greek & Roman Antiquities*. December 11, 1991. New York.

Overbeck, B. and Meshorer, Y. 1993. *Das heilige Land: Antike Münzen und Siegel aus einem Jahrtausend jüdischer Geschichte*. Catalog der Sonderausstellung. München.

Parise, N.F. 1971. Per uno studio del sistema ponderale ugaritico. *DdA* 4–5:3–36.

Parise, N.F. 1981. Mina di Ugarit, mina di Karkemish, mina di Khatti. *DdA* 3:155–160.

PEQ — *Palestine Exploration Quarterly*.

Prignaud, J. 1970. Notes d'épigraphie hébraique. *RB* 77:50–67.

Pritchard, J. 1959. *Hebrew Inscriptions and Stamps from Gibeon*. Philadelphia.

Ramat Raḥel — Aharoni, Y. (et al.) 1964. *Excavations at Ramat Raḥel, Seasons 1961 and 1962*. Roma.

RB — *Revue Biblique*.

Reifenberg, A. 1954. Hebrew Seals and Stamps. *IEJ* 4:139–142.

Renz J. and Röllig W. 1995. *Handbuch der Althebräischen Epigraphic* Bd. I, II1, III, Darmstadt.

Ronzevalle , S. 1926. Note sur le texte phénicien de la fléche publiee par M.P.E. Guigues, *MUSJ* 11:329–358.

RSO — *Rivista degli Studi Orientali*.

Sachau, W. 1986. Aramäische Inschriften, *Sitsungsberichte der preussischen Akademie der Wissenschaften* 41:1051–1064.

Sader, H. 1990. Deux épigraphes phéniciennes inedites. La pointe de fléche. *Syria* 67:215–218.

Sass, B. 1988. The Genesis of the Alphabet and its Development in the Second Millennium B.C. *Agypten und Altes Testament* 13. Wiesbaden.

SdT 1980 — *Sauvegarde de Tyr*, Unesco, Exposition "Tyr a travers les ages" 14.

SEL — *Studi Epigrafici e Linguistici.*

Sellers, O.R. 1993. *The Citadel of Beth Zur.* Philadelphia.

Shoham, Y. 1994. A Group of Hebrew Bullae from Yigal Shiloh's Excavations in the City of David, in: Geva, H. (ed.) *Ancient Jerusalem Revealed.* Jerusalem.

Sokoloff, M. 1992. *A Dictionary of Jewish Palestine Aramaic of the Byzantine Period.* Ramat-Gan.

Stamm, J.J. 1980. *Beiträge zur hebräischen und altorientalischen Namenkunde*, ed. Jenni E. and Klopfenstein. (*OBO* 30). Fribourg and Göttingen.

Starcky, J. 1982. La fléche de Zakarbaʿal, roi d'Amurru. *Archéologie au Levant.* Recueil Roger Saidah. Paris:179–186.

Stern, E. 1962. Midot umišqalot (Measures and Weights) *EB* 4:846–878.

Stern, E. 1982. *Material Culture of the Land of the Bible in the Persian Period 538–332 B.C.* Warminster.

Sternberg, F and Wolfe, L. 1989. *Objects with Semitic Inscriptions, 1100 B.C.–700 A.D., Jewish, Early Christian and Byzantine Antiquities.* Auction XXIII. Zürich.

Sternberg, F. 1990. *Antike Münzen, Griechen — Römer — Byzantiner Phönizische Kleinkunst — Objekte mit Antiken Inschriften.* Auction XXIV. Zürich.

Tarragon, J.M. 1990. La pointe de fléche inscrite des Peres Blancs de Jerusalem. *RB* 99:245–251.

Timm, S. 1989. *Moab zwischen den Mächten. Studien zu historischen Denkmälern und Texten.* Wiesbaden. (on seals 159–264)

Torrey, C.C. 1940. A Hebrew Seal from the Reign of Aḥaz, *BASOR* 79:27–8.

UF — *Ugarit-Forschungen.*

Ussishkin, D. 1977. The Destruction of Lachish by Sennacherib and the Dating of the Royal Judean Storage Jars. *Tel-Aviv* 4:28–60.

Vattioni, F. 1969. I sigilli ebraici. *Biblica* 50:357–388.

Vaughn, A.G. 1996, *The Chronicler's Account of Ḥezekiah: The*

Relationship of Historical Data to a Theological Interpretation of 2 Chronicles 29–32. Ph.D dissertation, Princeton Theological Seminary.

Zadok, R. 1988. *The Pre-Hellenistic Israelite Anthroponymy and Prosopography*. Leuven.

Zsengeller, Y. 1996. Personal Names in the Wadi ed-Daliyeh Papyri. *Zeitschrift für Althebraistik* 9:182–189.

INDICES

a) Hebrew words

b) Phoenician words

c) Titles

d) Toponyms

e) Personal names

f) Numbers